The Perfected

Millennial

Kingdom

by

ROBERT L. MILLET

HAWKES PUBLISHING INC.
156 W. 2170 S. (Box 15711)
Salt Lake City, Utah 84115

Printing—Typesetting—Binding
by
HAWKES PUBLISHING INC.

—ACKNOWLEDGMENTS—

Grateful appreciation is expressed to the many friends and associates who have read this manuscript and offered helpful suggestions and encouragement. Thanks to my lovely wife Shauna, for her extreme patience in a very busy time of compilation and writing, and to my sweet daughter Angela, are also in order. Much appreciation is extended to Bob and Roy, stalwarts in preparing for the Millennial Kingdom. Finally, the writer is extremely grateful to Dr. Hyrum L. Andrus, a great scholar-teacher, who has inspired many with his original research and teachings concerning the socio-economic and political thought of the Prophet Joseph Smith.

Though this small project would not have been possible without the assistance of many others, I alone am responsible for the conclusions drawn from the evidence cited.

Robert L. Millet
September, 1973

Dedicated to
Albert L. Millet

a faithful Latter-day Saint, and one devoted to the
establishment of the Kingdom of God.

–TABLE OF CONTENTS–

TABLE OF CONTENTS cont.

TABLE OF CONTENTS cont.

KEY TO ABBREVIATION OF TITLES:

CR	CONFERENCE REPORTS
D&C	DOCTRINE AND COVENANTS
DHC	DOCUMENTARY HISTORY OF THE CHURCH
DEN	DESERET EVENING NEWS
DN	DESERET NEWS
IE	IMPROVEMENT ERA
JD	JOURNAL OF DISCOURSES
JI	JUVENILE INSTRUCTOR
TPJS	TEACHINGS OF THE PROPHET JOSEPH SMITH

In the abbreviated references, the numbers refer to the volume and page number, if separated by a colon. Thus, DHC 5:555 refers to the Documentary History of the Church, volume 5 and page 555 of that volume.

All references are direct quotations, except when ellipses (. . . .) indicate that some material has been left out, or where brackets [ ] indicate that the author has added words not in the original source.

—INTRODUCTION—

What is the Kingdom of God? Is it only a Church? Will this Kingdom eventually meet every human need? These and other related questions are treated directly in this short work. This book aims at a brief synthesis of the full program of the Lord's Kingdom, as envisioned by the Modern Seer, Joseph Smith. It is an attempt to consider the many facets of the Kingdom of God and the ways in which this divine organization will ultimately give the answer to every social problem of the present day. Each of the chapters of this work aims specifically at answering vital questions in the minds of many pondering Latter-day Saints: What is Zion? What is the relationship between the Society of Zion and the Kingdom of God? What are some socio-economic principles operating in a society of the pure in heart? How does the Government of God really operate, as compared to our present political institutions? What are we doing now in the Church to prepare for the full program of the Kingdom? What are some things that must shortly come to pass in order to begin final preparations for such an establishment?

A thoughtful search of the pages that follow will give to the reader a more meaningful understanding of the Lord's total plan for the salvation and exaltation of the righteous. It will also give to the reader a greater appreciation for the supplication of the Savior in the Meridian of Time: "Thy kingdom come. Thy will be done in earth, as it is in heaven." (Matthew 6:10)

SYNOPSIS OF CONTENT

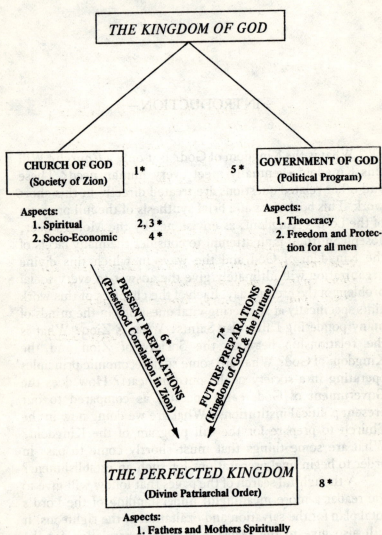

THE KINGDOM OF GOD

CHURCH OF GOD
(Society of Zion)

1*   5*

GOVERNMENT OF GOD
(Political Program)

Aspects:
1. Spiritual   2, 3 *
2. Socio-Economic   4 *

Aspects:
1. Theocracy
2. Freedom and Protection for all men

PRESENT PREPARATIONS
(Priesthood Correlation in Zion)   6*

FUTURE PREPARATIONS
(Kingdom of God & the Future)   7*

THE PERFECTED KINGDOM
(Divine Patriarchal Order)   8*

Aspects:
1. Fathers and Mothers Spiritually
2. Kings and Priests unto God

---

* indicates the specific chapter number

Call upon the Lord, that his kingdom may go forth upon the earth, that the inhabitants thereof may receive it, and be prepared for the days to come, in the which the Son of Man shall come down in heaven, clothed in the brightness of his glory, to meet the kingdom of God which is set up on the earth.

Wherefore, may the kingdom of God go forth, that the kingdom of heaven may come, that thou, O God, mayest be glorified in heaven so on earth, that thine enemies may be subdued; for thine is the honor, power and glory, forever and ever.

—Joseph Smith

CHAPTER 1

THE ZION CONCEPT

WHAT IS ZION?

Exactly what do we mean when we speak of Zion? This is a difficult question to answer directly, for Zion means many things to many people. There are, however, certain limitations that should be observed in speaking of the concept of Zion: Zion should not be used in everyday conversation to refer to everything lovely or seemingly sacred, for as we continue to overuse this meaningful concept in our everyday speech, much of its original beauty and true signification is gradually lost. In the discussion which follows, five related but specifically different connotations of Zion in Latter-day Saint culture will be considered.

Zion originally referred to Mount Zion in Jerusalem. By extension, people gradually began to refer to the entire city of Jerusalem as Zion. Jerusalem is the same city as Salem, the city of peace which Melchizedek helped to transform into a haven of perfect unity in all socio-economic and religious matters.[1] During the time that David and Solomon reigned as kings, Jerusalem prospered and gained great acclaim. It was in Jerusalem that the majestic Temple of Solomon was built. After the Kingdom was divided in 975 B.C., Jerusalem remained the capital of the smaller Kingdom of Judah.[2]

A second sense in which Zion is used in scripture and everyday conversation is in reference to the establishment of God's people as a body in the tops of the Rocky Mountains. The Prophets Micah and Isaiah saw a similar vision, and their descriptions of this gathering were practically identical. After predicting the desolation of Mount Zion and Jerusalem in general, Micah describes his prophetic vision:

> *But in the last days it shall come to pass that the mountain of the House of the Lord shall be established in the top of the mountains, and it shall be exalted above the hills; and people shall flow unto it.*
>
> *And many nations shall come, and say, Come and let us go up to the mountain of the Lord, and to the house of the God of Jacob; and he will teach us of his ways, and we will walk in his paths: for the law shall go forth out of Zion, and the word of the Lord from Jerusalem.*[3]

It is to this Zion that the Saints of God will gather in the times of national and international disruption; it is to this Zion that the honorable men of the earth will flee for protection and security.

A third connotation of Zion refers to the establishment of a city system known as the New Jerusalem.[4] The Lord gave us to understand by revelation that the center place of this order will be located at Independence (Jackson County), Missouri.[5] This Zion will be the societal structure that is established in the last days, just prior to the Savior's Second Advent in glory, and that which will serve as the source of a theocratic world government. Zion will become an ensign and a standard to the world, because of its stability and union in an era of universal chaos.[6]

Fourth, Zion is often used to refer to those groups of people through the ages who have managed to sanctify themselves as a group and obtain heaven. The people of Enoch, Melchizedek, the Saints in America after the visit of Christ, and some of the Hebrew Saints are among the many groups who applied the divine teaching and philosophy necessary to rend the veil, establish social stability and unity, and maintain the pure love of Christ throughout the entire society. Many of these societies obtained the righteous power of faith and priesthood to such a degree as to be able to leave behind a wicked world and be taken into the rest of God. [7] The evidence seems to indicate that the Lord has taken Zion from all His creations; that is, at least one body of righteous beings on each creation has managed to flee to the abode of God. [8] Elder Orson Pratt made this declaration concerning Zion:

> *Notwithstanding the unnumbered worlds which have been created,* out of each one of these creations the Lord had taken Zion *(in other words a people called Zion) to his own bosom. . . . I mention these things to show that we have, in the revelations that God has given, many indications, that there are worlds beside our own that are fallen; also that we may see that the Lord has one grand method, for the salvation of the righteous of all worlds— that Zion is selected and taken from all of them.* [9]

A final sense is that in which Zion refers to a righteous state of being or mind. Thus the Lord told Joseph Smith by revelation that Zion is ''the pure in heart.'' [10] In this case, Zion represents a people or group of people whose hearts have been made pure and clean by the regenerating powers of the Holy Ghost. To be *in* Zion is to be among the pure in heart. Therefore Zion is both the pure in heart (the people) and where the pure in heart dwell (the place). In a similar way, President Brigham Young spoke of one having the ''Spirit of Zion:''

> *. . . unless the people live before the Lord in the obedience of his commandments, they cannot have Zion within them. They must carry it with them if they expect to live in it, to enjoy it, and increase in it. . . as to the*

spirit of Zion, *it is in the hearts of the Saints, of those who love and serve the Lord with all their might, mind, and strength.* [11]

President Young later said:

Zion will be redeemed and built up, and the Saints will rejoice. This is the land of Zion; and who are Zion? The pure in heart are Zion; they have Zion within them. Purify yourselves, sanctify the Lord God in your hearts, and have the Zion of God within you, *and then you will rejoice more and more.*[12]

More directly, if Zion *is* the pure in heart, and the pure in heart are those who shall see God,[13] then Zion consists of a society of people grounded in the blessings of the Second Comforter.[14]

ZION SOCIETIES IN TIMES PAST

A careful study of the scriptures reveals very clearly that many noble Saints since the beginning have been successful in coping with the problems of society and establishing perfect order and unity among the people. The following section is aimed at viewing some of these societies and discussing what it was that made them true Zion Societies.

ENOCH AND HIS CITY.

Of all the sons of God, the Prophet Enoch stands among the greatest. The seventh from Adam, Enoch was called to preach to and prepare a people while a relatively young man. Perhaps the most beautiful description of Enoch's spiritual preparation and readiness was given by Joseph Young, brother of Brigham Young. He spoke of Enoch as being—

> *predisposed from his infancy to accept of everything that*
> *was revealed from God; and it being instinctively in-*
> *corporated in his very nature to be eligible to every divine*
> *manifestation. he finally grew to be a God in humanity,*
> *and he received this testimony from his heavenly Father*
> *that he pleased him.* [15]

At least three salient points in President Joseph Young's statement about Enoch need some amplification. First of all, Enoch was described as one ''predisposed from his infancy to accept of everything that was revealed from God.'' This seems to indicate the quality of perfect faith in Enoch from the time of early childhood; he is thus characterized as one whose whole soul delights in fulfilling the desires of the Almighty. Closely tied with this first characteristic of Enoch is the fact that he was of such spiritual calibre that it was ''... instinctively incorporated in his very nature to be eligible to every divine manifestation.'' In other words, it appears that since Enoch's entire system yearned for the things of the Spirit, he thus was perfectly capable of receiving the greatest of God's manifestations, including the transcendent blessings of the Second Comforter. This truth is born out by the following scriptures:

And *Enoch walked with God* after he begat Methuselah three hundred years, and begat sons and daughters:
And all the days of Enoch were three hundred and sixty five years:
And *Enoch walked with God:* and he was not; for God took him. [16]
And *Enoch talked with the Lord:* and he said unto the Lord: surely Zion shall dwell in safety forever. But the Lord said unto Enoch: Zion have I blessed, but the residue of the people have I cursed. [17]
And *Enoch and all his people walked with God,* and he dwelt in the midst of Zion; and it came to pass that Zion was not, for God received it up into his own bosom; and from thence went forth the saving, ZION IS FLED. [18]

The final characteristic of Enoch worth noting is that "... he finally grew to be a God in humanity." This has reference to the fact that Enoch grew in spiritual matters to the point where he made his calling and election sure to eternal life in the flesh and received the fulness of Priesthood powers:[19] he was thus a God.[20]

Concerning Enoch's missionary labors to the people and his work in ultimately bringing them to a point of sanctification, Elder Orson Pratt said:

> *Enoch was called of God when but a young man, and was sent forth unto the antedeluvian nations to preach faith, repentance, and baptism for the remission of sins, and to prophesy and warn the people of approaching judgement. Many among the nations hearkened unto his voice, and received the gospel, and became the sons of God; for the Holy Ghost fell unto them and they were born of God. These, by the commandment of God, were gathered out from the nations by themselves, and they were established upon the high places of the earth, and upon the mountains, and became sanctified before the Lord; "And the Lord came and dwelt with His people, and they dwelt in righteousness. The fear of the Lord was upon all nations, so great was the glory of the Lord which was upon his people."*
>
> *It was under these circumstances that the Lord called this people Zion.*[21]

President Brigham Young stated that Enoch and his city had gained power over the elements of the earth, and had the Spirit of the Lord to such an extent that they took their portion of the earth (including land, houses, and animals) and left the earth.[22] Likewise, the Prophet Joseph taught that Enoch's people applied a "divine philosophy." Said the Prophet:

> *... the people, and the city, and the foundations of the earth on which it stood, had partaken of so much of the*

immortal elements, bestowed upon them by God through the teachings of Enoch, that it became philosophically impossible for them to remain any longer upon the earth; consequently, Enoch and his people, with the city which they occupied, and the foundations on which it stood, with a large piece of earth immediately connected with all the foundations and the city, had assumed an aerial position within the limits of our solar system; and this in consequence of their faith. [23]

Joseph Smith further taught when Enoch and his people do descend to meet Zion on earth at the coming of the Lord, that the city of Enoch would again take its place in the same area of the earth from which it had been detached, namely that area now forming the Gulf of Mexico. [24] This, the most classic example of Zion Society, provides the basis for our understanding of many of the principles to be applied in establishing a perfect order.

Even after Enoch and his city had been translated, there were many who accepted the gospel and became powerful in their faith, even as the people of Enoch. In vision, Enoch ". . . beheld angels descending out of heaven, bearing testimony of the Father and Son; and the Holy Ghost fell on many, and they were caught up by the powers of heaven into Zion." [25] Thus it appears that many Saints after the time of Enoch sanctified themselves and were therefore worthy to join Enoch and his people in the bosom of God.

MELCHIZEDEK AND THE PEOPLE OF SALEM.

Perhaps the greatest thing that might be remembered in evaluating the magnitude of the man Melchizedek is the fact that the Church of his day (under the direction of the Lord) called the Priesthood of God after his name. [26] The Prophet Alma gave a description of this great man of God, and ended his description with a marvelous tribute:

> *Now this Melchizedek was a King over the land of Salem; and his people had waxed strong in iniquity and abomination; yea, they had all gone astray; they were full of all manner of wickedness;*
>
> *But Melchizedek having exercised mighty faith, and received the office of the high priesthood after the holy order of God, did preach repentance unto his people, and behold, they did repent; and Melchizedek did establish peace in the land in his days; therefore he was called the prince of peace, for he was the king of Salem; and he did reign under his father.*
>
> *Now,* there were many before him, and also there were many afterwards, but none were greater; *therefore of him they have more particularly made mention.*[27]

Thus Melchizedek was a great Patriarch, being both a High Priest to the people, as well as serving as political King.[28] In other words, Melchizedek held keys necessary to preside over the Church and also the keys to preside as King, both rights centering in him. The King James Translation of the Bible states that Father Abraham was blessed by Melchizedek, and also that Melchizedek was the man to whom Abraham paid tithes (again showing Melchizedek's position as head of the Church.)[29] The Prophet Joseph Smith further taught that this King of Salem had power and authority over Abraham, holding the "keys and powers of endless life."[30] Melchizedek thus held the keys of the Patriarchal Order necessary to grant unto people an assurance of their exaltations. Undoubtedly, Abraham received the keys of the Partriarchal Priesthood from Melchizedek. In this way, the promises of God to Abraham were fulfilled.

Mechizedek, being mighty in the power of the Spirit, was able to influence the city of Salem to such a degree that Zion was again established on earth. Joseph Smith's Inspired Revision of Genesis makes possible the following insights:

Now Melchizedek was a man of faith, who wrought righteousness; and when a child he feared God, and stopped the mouths of lions and quenched the violence of fire.

And thus, having been approved of God, he was ordained an high priest after the order of the covenant which God made with Enoch. . . .

For God having sworn unto Enoch and unto his seed with an oath by himself; that every one being ordained after this order and calling should have power, by faith, to break mountains, to divide the seas, to dry up waters, to turn them out of their course;

And men having this faith, coming up unto this order of God, were translated and taken into heaven.

And now, Melchizedek was a priest of this order; therefore he obtained peace in Salem, and was called the prince of peace.

And his people wrought righteousness, and obtained heaven, and sought for the city of Enoch which God had before taken, *having reserved it unto the latter days, or the end of the world. . . .* [32]

From the above it would appear (though we are not certain) that Melchizedek and the city of Salem were translated, and thus "obtained heaven," even as the city of Enoch.

ZION IN AMERICA.

After the visit of the Savior among the ancient inhabitants of America, the people of this Western Hemisphere enjoyed an era of peace and union for almost two hundred years.[33] The Holy Spirit was poured out in rich abundance upon all, such that the pure love of Christ permeated the entire land. Strifes, envyings, and turmoil were nowhere to be found, because of the powerful refining forces of the Holy Ghost. Being filled with that Spirit which prompts man to deal justly with his neighbor,[34] the people of America thus entered into social unions and covenant relationships with each other. The people consecrated all into a common fund and received according to their needs, wants, and abilities. There were no poor among them, but all were part of a divine socio-economic program that insured total equality and freedom.[35] The record informs us further that the Spirit of the Lord rested upon the people of the land in such a mighty way that all were made "partakers of the heavenly gift," and that the working of miracles was very characteristic of the day.[36]

The tragedy of this Zion people is that the perfect order did not last. By the year 201 A.D. the Lord had prospered the people greatly because of their righteousness and unity. But as is so often the case, the men and women began to be lifted up in pride, insomuch that the Saints no longer had things in common, and the blessed state of unity gradually dissolved. Zion in America was no more.[37]

THE HEBREW CHURCH.

Following Christ's death and ascension in Jerusalem, the remaining followers joined together in an attempt to solidify the ties among the Christians. The fourth chapter of Acts tells us that after a mighty prayer together, the Saints were filled with the Holy Ghost; being thus imbued with this divine influence they were of one mind and one heart:[38] they desired to enter into the Law of Consecration, in order that all might be one socially, economically, and spiritually. These Saints thus attained heaven on earth, as had many who had preceded them in earlier dispensations of the gospel. The author of the Book of Acts describes the subsequent outpourings of the Spirit very simply: ". . .and great grace (i.e., divine endowments of light and power) was upon them all."[39] The Prophet Joseph was much more explicit in describing the heavenly gifts that were bestowed upon the Hebrew Saints because of their oneness and equality. He spoke of their condition as having come . . .*unto the spirits of just men made perfect, and unto an innumberable company of angels, unto God the*

Father of all, and to Jesus Christ the Mediator of the new covenant.'' [40]

And thus we get some idea of the types of Zion societies that have existed in ages past. A careful and ponderous study of these peoples will bring us close to an understanding of what is necessary in order to attain Zion.

SUMMARY

The concept of ''Zion'' is and has been a changing one, mainly because of the different connotations of the term. Zion may be used in conversation to refer to at least five different (yet related) concepts: (1) The city of Jerusalem; (2) The mountain of the Lord's house referred to in prophetic vision by Micah and Isaiah; (3) The New Jerusalem or Society of Zion to be established in a day just prior to the Second Advent; (4) Zion Societies in times past which have ''obtained heaven;'' and (5) A righteous state of being, characterized by a people which are pure in heart.

A close study of the scriptures reveals the fact that many of the Lord's children have been successful in solving the problems of society and thus establishing cultural unity and equality. Examples of these types of societies include (1) Enoch and his city; (2) Melchizedek and the people of Salem; (3) The inhabitants of America just after the Savior's visit; and (4) the Hebrew Church. All of these peoples represent that goal toward which we should and must aspire if we are to restore Zion once again to the earth.

CHAPTER 1
—FOOTNOTES—

1. The reign of Melchizedek in Salem will be considered later in this chapter.
2. For a more detailed description of Jerusalem, see Talmage's *Articles of Faith*, pp. 347-348.
3. Micah 4:1-2; Isaiah 2:2-3.
4. See Revelation 21; 3 Nephi 21; Ether 13:3-8; Moses 7:62.

5. D&C 57:3; See also a statement by Orson Pratt in JD 15:365.
6. D&C 45:70; D&C 64:42-43. For a more detailed description of the socio-economic and political programs of the Kingdom, see Chapters 4 and 5.
7. See Moses 7:21, 69; I.V. Genesis 14:26-34; JD 3:320.
8. Moses 7:64.
9. JD 19:293.
10. D&C 97:21.
11. JD 2:253; see also *Ibid.*, 8:205.
12. *Ibid.*, 8:193; see also *Ibid.*, 1:3-4.
13. Matthew 5:8; 3 Nephi 12:8; D&C 67:10; D&C 93:1.
14. A brief discussion of the Second Comforter and its blessings will be undertaken in Chapter 3.
15. Joseph Young, "Enoch and His City," in *History of the Organization of the Seventies,* Deseret News Steam Printing Establishment, 1878, p. 9.
16. Genesis 5:22-24.
17. Moses 7:20.
18. *Ibid.*, 7:69.
19. To fully appreciate the fact that making one's calling and election sure gives one the fulness of the priesthood, compare statements by the Prophet Joseph Smith on TPJS, p. 337 and TPJS, p. 338. See also D&C 76:53-57.
20. D&C 132:19-20; D&C 76:56-58.
21. Orson Pratt, *The Seer,* II (May, 1854), p. 262.
22. JD 3:320.
23. Young, *op. cit.,* p. 11.
24. *Ibid.*, p. 12.
25. Moses 7:27.
26. D&C 107:2-4.
27. Alma 13:17-19.
28. The Patriarchal Order of the priesthood will be discussed in Chapter 8.
29. Hebrews 5:1-2.
30. TPJS, p. 322.
31. *Ibid.*, pp. 322-323.
32. I.V. Genesis 14:26-27, 30, 32-34.
33. 4 Nephi.
34. D&C 11:12.
35. See 4 Nephi 3. A more thorough discussion of the Law of Consecration and Stewardship will be undertaken in Chapter 4.
36. 4 Nephi 3, 5.
37. *Ibid.*, 24-26.
38. Acts 4:31-37.
39. *Ibid.*, 4:33.
40. TPJS, p. 325.

CHAPTER 2

INITIAL PREPARATIONS FOR ZION

On earth man finds himself in a fallen state, alienated and shut out from the Father of spirits. Having suffered a spiritual death with the Fall of our first parents, man is left to struggle in an attempt to regain the paradisiacal state before the Fall. The spiritual aspect of the Society of Zion is that part of the Church which aids man in his spiritual maturation; only through the ordinances and powers of the gospel (which center in the Atonement of Christ) can man ever hope to rise from the natural state to the spiritual. The assurance of eternal life is not gained overnight, but rather is gained at the end of a long process of spiritual growth. This chapter will discuss part of this divine process of gaining eternal life through the principles of Justification and Sanctification.

JUSTIFICATION

If we leave the gospel context to define Justification in a general way, we find that to justify means to exonerate or remove all reason for restitution; it means also to make right in the eyes of a lawful body. If we now turn to the gospel setting, we find that to justify means to make right with God, or to cleanse one sufficiently to bear the glory of God. Initially, baptism and the reception of the Holy Ghost are the means by which the individual reaches the justified state. After sincere repentance, the act of baptism serves as a visible witness to God and man of a sacred covenant relationship made and entered into. As an ordinance, baptism symbolizes the crucifixion of the old self, the washing of the body and spirit, and the rise into a newness of life. After receiving the Holy Ghost and having the sins removed,[1] the new candidate for the Kingdom stands clean and pure, and is thus in a state of justification; the demands of justice have no claims on the person at that moment. Only after the person turns again to sin does he leave the justified state and thus leave himself open to the demands of universal justice. Our greatest concern should thus be how one may become justified to God again after sinning since baptism.

OBTAINING AND RETAINING A REMISSION OF SINS.

The process of obtaining a remission of sins after baptism is exactly the same as before baptism, with the exception of the ordinance of baptism itself. Man must exercise saving faith in the blood of Christ.

> *Therefore being justified by faith, we have peace with God through our Lord Jesus Christ:*
> *By whom also we have access by faith unto this grace wherein we stand, and rejoice in hope of the glory of God.* [2]

With saving faith comes the repentance process. A major factor involved in the forgiveness of sins is the keeping of the commandments by the repentant soul.[3] By this means, the individual is able to witness outwardly his full desires for fellowship among the just. That a remission of sins is granted to members of the Church many years after baptism is clear from the scriptures. In a revelation to Joseph Smith and six Elders at Fayette, the Lord declared in September of 1830:

> *Behold, verily, verily, I say unto you, that at this time* your sins are forgiven you, *therefore ve receive these things; but remember to sin no more, lest perils shall come upon you.* [4]

A similar declaration was given to Joseph Smith and the Elders in September of 1831:

> *Behold, thus saith the Lord your God unto you, O ye Elders of my church, hearken ye and hear, and receive my will concerning you.*
>
> *For verily I say unto you, I will that ye should overcome the world; wherefore I will have compassion upon you.*
>
> *There are those among you who have sinned; but verily I say, for this once, for mine own glory, and for the salvation of souls, I have forgiven you your sins.* [5]

When Christ appeared to Joseph Smith and Oliver Cowdery in the Kirtland Temple on April 3, 1836, He spoke as follows:

> *I am the first and the last; I am he who liveth, I am he who was slain; I am your advocate with the Father.*
>
> *Behold,* your sins are forgiven you; *you are clean before me; therefore, lift up your heads and rejoice.* [6]

After one has been forgiven his sins and is made pure once again, he must then fight the battle of remaining in a justified state. Since all sin at least inadvertently, there must be some method of retaining a remission of sins from day to day. King Benjamin spoke to this very question in his marvelous discourse in the fourth Chapter of Mosiah.

And again I say unto you as I have said before, that as ye have come to the knowledge of the glory of God, or if ye have known of his goodness and have tasted of his love, and have received a remission of your sins, which causeth such exceeding great joy in your souls, even so I would that ye should remember, and always retain in remembrance, the greatness of God, and your own nothingness, and his goodness and long-suffering towards you, unworthy creatures, and humble yourselves even in the depths of humility, calling on the name of the Lord daily, and standing steadfastly in the faith of that which is to come, which was spoken by the mouth of the angel.

And behold, I say unto you that if ye do this ye shall always rejoice, and be filled with the love of God, and always retain a remission of your sins; *and ye shall grow in the knowledge of the glory of him that created you, or in the knowledge of that which is just and true.*

And ye will not have a mind to injure one another, but to live peaceably, and to render to every man according to that which is his due.

And now, for the sake of these things which I have spoken unto you—that is, for the sake of retaining a remission of your sins from day to day, *that ye may walk guiltless before God—*I would that ye should impart of your substance to the poor, *every man according to that which he hath, such as feeding the hungry, clothing the naked, visiting the sick and administering to their relief, both spiritually and temporally, according to their wants.* [7]

It might be valuable to enumerate the specific points which King Benjamin felt were necessary in order to retain a remission of sins. *First,* he suggested that the people should always remember the greatness of God and their total nothingness without Him. *Second,* they should strive to remain humble. *Third,* they should stand steadfastly in their faith in the coming Messiah. *Fourth,* they should live peacefully among their fellow men. *Fifth,* they should administer to the spiritual and temporal welfare of their neighbors. This last principle involves living the Law of the Gospel, and thus living outside oneself. The Prophet Joseph summarizes the situation by stating that "To be justified before God we must love one another: we must overcome evil; we must visit the fatherless and the widows in their affliction, and we must keep ourselves unspotted from the world." [8]

SANCTIFICATION

The man in a justified state stands in a new relationship to the Master, Jesus Christ. Being pure and clean, he is a fit vessel through which the Lord may work should He choose to do so. Having received the Holy Spirit into his life, he is prepared for the working of spiritual gifts for the conversion and edification of others. Having renovated his soul through repentance and the cleansing powers of the Holy Ghost, his outlook on life takes on new dimensions. He is on the path to Sanctification.

CONDITIONS OF THE SANCTIFIED.

In order to examine the state of Sanctification more closely, we will consider some scriptural statements or accounts that are descriptive of the sanctified. In speaking of Sanctification, Elder Orson Hyde said:

> . . . *it means a purification of, or a* putting away from, us, as individuals and as a community, everything that is evil, *or that is not in accordance with the mind and will of our Heavenly Father.*
>
> *Sanctification has also an eye to our own preservation for usefulness—for executing, carrying forward, and perpetuating the work of the most high God.* [9]

Elder Hyde emphasizes that Sanctification is the purification of the individual and the society. He suggests that this state is to be attained only as we put away from us, individually and collectively, things of an evil nature. He also emphasizes another aspect of Sanctification which is of great value. He speaks of the spiritual "survival value" which Sanctification has; only as we become sanctified may we be totally useful in executing the Divine Will. In a similar vein, President Brigham Young said that Sanctification consists—

> . . . in overcoming every sin and bringing all in subjection to the law of Christ. *God has placed in us a pure spirit; when this reigns predominant, without let or hindrance, and triumphs over the flesh and rules and governs and controls as the Lord controls the heavens and the earth, this I call the blessing of sanctification.*[10]

The Prophet suggests to us that Sanctification entails overcoming every sin. This appears to be a gigantic (if not impossible) task at first glance. Yet, if we turn to the "Vision of the Glories," we find that one of the descriptions of those who are Celestial is that they "shall overcome all things."[11] We are also instructed that Sanctification exists when the spirit in man reigns predominant over the flesh. When the battle between spirit and body is resolved and the soul thus acts in unison, this we call the sanctified state.

In the 51st year of the reign of the Judges (or about 41 B.C.) we read about the condition of some of the Nephites:

> . . . *they did fast and pray oft, and did wax stronger and stronger in their humility, and firmer and firmer in the faith of Christ, unto the filling their souls with joy and consolation, yea, even to the purifying and the sanctification of their hearts,* which sanctification cometh because of their yielding their hearts unto God.[12]

We receive wise counsel from the Lord in the 88th Section of the *Doctrine and Covenants* as follows:

And if your eye be single to my glory, your whole bodies shall be filled with light, and there shall be no darkness in you; and that body which is filled with light comprehendeth all things.

Therefore, sanctify yourselves that your minds become single to God, *and the days will come that you shall see him; for he will unveil his face unto you. . . .* [13]

The two preceding scriptural accounts are closely related. The sanctified person seems to have "yielded his heart unto God," and has "an eye single to the glory of God." To yield our hearts unto God is to put ourselves in the spiritual frame of mind such that we understand clearly the purposes and designs of God. It is to pray that the Father will plant within our hearts His desires, and to work so that our will is swallowed up in His. To have our eye single to the glory of God is to have our lives structured and our aspirations centered so that our ultimate desire is to aid in bringing to pass the immortality and eternal life of man. [14]

A final condition of the sanctified for us to consider is best illustrated by the following scriptural account of the Saints in the early history of the world:

> *Therefore they were called after this holy order, and were sanctified, and their garments were washed white through the blood of the Lamb.*
> *Now they, after being sanctified by the Holy Ghost, having their garments made white, being pure and spotless before God,* could not look upon sin save it were with abhorrence. . . . [15]

These people had developed the powers of the Spirit in their lives to such an extent that the very thought of sin caused them to cringe and shudder.

SANCTIFICATION THROUGH THE BLOOD OF CHRIST.

It is impossible for man to sanctify himself. Only through an active acceptance of the powers of the Atonement may one ever hope to be glorified in Christ as Christ is in the Father. The indescribable suffering and anguish in Gethsemane is the basis for salvation in the Lord. By some strange and incomprehensible means, the shedding of blood by the Savior in the Garden provides the path to eternal life. Those who repent and call on Him are cleansed by His atoning blood.

> *And no unclean thing can enter into his kingdom: therefore nothing entereth into his rest save it be* those who have washed their garments in my blood, *because of their faith, and the repentance of all their sins, and their faithfulness unto the end.* [16]

Again, let us recall an earlier description of some sanctified individuals:

> *Therefore they were called after this holy order, and were sanctified, and their garments were washed white through the blood of the Lamb.* [17]

So it is only through the "precious blood of Christ, as of a lamb without blemish and without spot" [18] that persons are sanctified and made holy.

THE HOLY GHOST AS SANCTIFIER.

We speak a great deal of the Holy Ghost in his role as revelator, but often forget another of his major roles: that of sanctifier. Though we become sanctified through the blood of Jesus Christ, the active agent through which the Sanctification process is accomplished is the Holy Ghost. He is the purger, the renovator, the purifier. It is by his actions that bodies are renewed, [19] and bodies are filled with light.[20] Scriptural accounts showing the Holy Ghost to be the active agent in Sanctification are numerous, but we will only consider two examples here. Alma, in counseling the members of the Church said:

> *Yea, will ye persist in supposing that ye are better one than another; yea, will ye persist in the persecution of your brethren, who humble themselves and do walk after the holy order of God, wherewith they have been brought into this church, having been* sanctified by the Holy Spirit, *and they do bring forth works which are meet for repentance. . . .*[21]

The next passage is one which we have already considered, but one which we will now view in another context.

> *Now they,* after being sanctified by the Holy Ghost, *having their garments made white, being pure and spotless before God, could not look upon sin save it were with abhorrence.*[22]

SANCTIFICATION AND JUSTIFICATION: A CONTRAST.

One may ask the question at this point: "If Justification is the removal of sins and the process of making one 'right' with God, and Sanctification is the process of becoming pure and holy by means of the cleansing actions of the Holy Ghost, then how do these two processes really differ?" This is a valid question, as the difference between the justified person and the sanctified person seems, at this point, to be unclear. An aid in making this important distinction is to remember that Justification has reference to the removal of sins, whereas Sanctification has reference to the removal of the *effects* of sin. This point is elaborated beautifully in the following remarks by Elder Orson Pratt:

Without the aid of the Holy Ghost, a person who has long been accustomed to love sin, and whose affections and desires have long run with delight in the degraded channel of vice, would have but very little power to change his mind, at once, from its habituated course, and to walk in newness of life. Though his sins may have been cleansed away, yet so great is the force of habit, that he would, without being renewed by the Holy Ghost, be easily overcome, and contaminated with sin. *Hence, it is infinitely important that the affections and desires should be, in a measure, changed and renewed, so as to cause him to hate that which he before loved, and to love that which he before hated. To thus renew the mind of man is the work of the Holy Ghost.* [23]

SUMMARY

The Gospel of Christ is the divine power whereby man may climb from his fallen state on earth to a spiritual state, enjoying the gifts and powers of the Holy Ghost. Man is *justified* as he obtains a remission of his sins and thus makes himself right with God. He retains a remission of sins through service to his fellow man. To be *sanctified* is to have overcome the effects of sin; the man in the sanctified state has no more desire for evil, but seeks only righteousness. This person has yielded his heart unto God, and thus has an eye single to the glory of the Master. He is on the road to eternal life.

CHAPTER 2
—FOOTNOTES—

1. See 2 Nephi 31:17 as evidence that the Holy Ghost is the agent through which sins are removed.
2. Romans 5:1-2.
3. Moroni 8:25; D&C 76:52.
4. D&C 29:3.
5. *Ibid.*, 64:1-3.
6. *Ibid.*, 110:4-5.
7. Mosiah 4:11, 12, 13, 26.
8. DHC 2:229.
9. JD 1:71.
10. *Ibid.* 5:173.
11. D&C 76:60.
12. Helaman 3:35.
13. D&C 88:67-68.
14. Moses 1:39.
15. Alma 13:10-12.
16. 3 Nephi 27:19.
17. Alma 13:11.
18. 1 Peter 1:19.
19. D&C 84:33.
20. *Ibid.*, 88:67.
21. Alma 5:54.
22. *Ibid.*, 13:12.
23. Orson Pratt, *The Holy Spirit* (Liverpool, 1856), pp. 56-57.

CHAPTER 3

THE PATH TO ETERNAL LIFE

SEALING

As man continues to hunger and thirst after righteousness, and to live by every word of God, he eventually receives the assurance that he will be exalted in the eternal worlds.[1]   To thus be sealed up unto eternal life is to receive the knowledge that one has met the challenge of mortality. This assurance may come while the individual is still in the flesh, or it may come after death. Thus the Lord declared in revelation that ''. . . if you keep my commandments and endure to the end you shall have eternal life, which gift is the greatest of all the gifts of God.''[2]   In discussing this subject, we will first attempt to define some of the related concepts and expressions that are associated with the doctrine of sealing. Next we will consider some of the revealed facts concerning those sealed unto eternal life.

THE HOLY SPIRIT OF PROMISE.
The Holy Spirit of Promise is the Holy Ghost.[3] When one is ''sealed by the Holy Spirit of Promise'' he is sealed up unto eternal life.[4]   Many in the Church are of the mistaken notion that an immediate sealing occurs when a couple are married by the priesthood in the Temple; this sealing in the Temple, however, is strictly contingent upon

righteousness. Joseph Smith taught that the Lord generally does not seal a man unto eternal life until the man has been thoroughly proved, and thus indicates by his actions that he is willing to serve God at all hazards.[5]   All covenants, bonds, contracts, and obligations entered into by the individual are then sealed, ratified, and receive the "stamp of approval" of the Holy Ghost. The scriptures reveal that a person must be sealed by the Holy Spirit of Promise before attaining Celestial glory; that is, the person must receive the assurance of eternal life before having the right to such. In speaking of those who are Celestial, the Lord said that these are they who ". . . overcome by faith, and are sealed by the Holy Spirit of Promise, which the Father sheds forth upon all those who are just and true."[6]

CALLING AND ELECTION.

The doctrine by which men are sealed unto eternal life has its basis in the doctrine of election. The doctrine of election has reference to the fact that every man or woman whose work on earth leads others to salvation was chosen and called to that position before the foundation of this world.[7]   When a person's calling and election is *made sure*, the blessings promised in the Grand Councils before mortality are realized in earth life. This involves the realization of the calling in the House of the Lord to become a King (Queen) and a Priest (Priestess) unto God in the Divine Patriarchal Order.

The doctrine of making one's calling and election sure to eternal life is a vital part of the Gospel of Christ, but one that has received little specific attention since the time of the Prophet Joseph Smith. It is unfortunate that such should be the case, for no doctrine gives more hope to the pure in heart than the doctrine which teaches, that man may receive the sure knowledge that he has place with the Father in Celestial glory. In speaking of making one's calling and election sure, Joseph Smith said:

> *This principle ought (in its proper place) to be taught, for God hath not revealed anything to Joseph, but what he will make known to the Twelve, and even to the least Saint may know all things as fast as he is able to bear them.* . . . [8]

THE MORE SURE WORD OF PROPHECY.

In instructions given to the Saints on May 17, 1843, the Prophet Joseph Smith explained that "The more sure word of prophecy means a man's knowing that he is sealed up unto eternal life, by revelation and the spirit of prophecy, through the power of the Holy Priesthood." [9]   A man receives this more sure word of prophecy, then, when he receives the knowledge, through the channels of the priesthood, that he is sealed unto eternal life. This seal may be broken only as one defiles his calling and commits the unpardonable sin. [10] For such a person, there is no repentance. [11]

The more sure word of prophecy also has its basis in the doctrine of election. In the Church we believe in the word of prophecy as the means by which men and women are called to positions in the Church. We are also taught, as has just been discussed, that the word of prophecy had its beginnings in the pre-earth councils. When a person on earth thus receives the calling that he had been elected or called to receive in the pre-earth existence, and receives the blessings it was prophesied he would obtain, he then has a *more sure* word of prophecy; it is the word of prophecy more sure than the contingent call he received in heaven. Instead of a man having the possibility of *becoming* a Patriarch (King and Priest), he *is* such.

THE SECOND COMFORTER.

Joseph Smith taught that after a man has thoroughly been proved, has received the more sure word of prophecy and thus made his calling and election sure, he may then receive Another Comforter:

> *Now what is this other Comforter? It is no more nor less than the Lord Jesus Christ Himself; and this is the sum and substance of the whole matter; that when any man obtains this last Comforter, he will have the personage of Jesus Christ to attend him, or appear unto him from time to time, and even He will manifest the Father unto him, and they will take up their abode with him, and the visions of the heavens will be opened unto him, and the Lord will teach him face to face, and he may have a perfect knowledge of the mysteries of the Kingdom of God. . . .* [12]

From the above we can see that the Second Comforter refers to the literal *presence* of the Son and the Father. But there is another way in which the expression "Second Comforter" is used in scripture. We read in a revelation given to Joseph Smith and the Elders in December of 1832, that the Second Comforter also refers to the *promise* of eternal life,[13] thus making it the same as the more sure word of prophecy. In a blessing to Vilate Kimball, wife of Heber C. Kimball, Patriarch Hyrum Smith said:

> *Beloved Sister: I lay my hands upon your head in the name of Jesus, and seal you unto eternal life— sealed here on earth and sealed in heaven, and your name written in the Lamb's Book of Life never to be blotted out.*
> *The same is mentioned and manifested to comfort your heart, and to be a comfort unto you hence forth and all your days. It is even a promise according to the mind of the Spirit, and the Spirit shall bear record of the truth;* the same is called the Second Comforter, not his presence, but his promise. *The same is as immutable as an oath by himself, because there is none greater, and there is no greater promise nor no greater blessing that can be given, and no greater riches, it being the riches of eternity, which are the greatest riches of all riches.* [14]

The blessings of the Second Comforter extend further to enable the worthy son of God to entertain other heavenly beings if the Lord wills it so. Joseph Smith taught that those who have made their calling and election sure have the right to commune with "an innumerable company of angels."[15] He further taught that those sealed unto eternal life have the privilege of receiving the spirits of just men made perfect to minister unto them.[16] Also, those who have met the mortal challenge completely may commune with the General Assembly and Church of the Firstborn.[17]

POWER TO SEAL INHERENT IN THE PRIESTHOOD.

There are many who have supposed that the sealing powers of the priesthood were not available until the coming of Elijah in 1836. That the sealing powers are inherent in the Melchizedek Priesthood restored by Peter, James, and John is evident from the following instructions of the Lord to the Elders as early as 1831:

> Go ye into all the world, preach the gospel to every creature, acting in the authority which I have given you, baptizing in the name of the Father, and of the Son, and of the Holy Ghost.
> And of as many as the Father shall bear record, to you shall be given power to seal them up unto eternal life. Amen.[18]

The powers to bind and loose on earth and in heaven are thus the same powers necessary to seal individuals unto eternal life.

DOCTRINE OF SEALING UNDERSTOOD IN THE HEBREW CHURCH.

The members of the Church at the time of Christ and after His resurrection were taught concerning being sealed unto eternal life; this is very evident from the writings of the early Apostles. In speaking of Christ to the Ephesians, Paul said:

> *In whom ye also trusted, after that ye heard the word*
> *of truth, the gospel of your salvation: in whom also after*
> *that ye believed,* ye were sealed with that holy Spirit of
> promise,
> *Which is the earnest of our inheritance until the*
> *redemption of the purchased possession, unto the praise*
> *of his glory.* [19]

Joseph Smith taught that Paul definitely had reference to a
man's making his calling and election sure.[20] Peter, in
enumerating a list of Godly qualities which lead to eternal
life, declared:

> *For if these things be in you, and abound, they make*
> *you that ye shall neither be barren nor unfruitful in the*
> *knowledge of our Lord Jesus Christ.*
> *But he that lacketh these things is blind, and cannot*
> *see afar off, and hath forgotten that he was purged from*
> *his old sins.*
> *Wherefore the rather, brethren,* give diligence to
> make your calling and election sure: *for if ye do these*
> *things, ye shall never fail:*
> *For so an entrance shall be ministered unto you*
> *abundantly into the everlasting kingdom of our Lord and*
> *Savior Jesus Christ.* [21]

In making reference to the glorious manifestation which the
Ancient Presidency had beheld on the Mount of Trans-
figuration, Peter continued in this same chapter:

> *For we have not followed cunningly devised fables,*
> *when we made known unto you the power and coming of*
> *our Lord Jesus Christ, but were eyewitnesses of his*
> *majesty.*
> *For he received from God the Father honour and*
> *glory, when there came such a voice to him from the*
> *excellent glory, This is my beloved Son, in whom I am*
> *well pleased.*

> *And this voice which came from heaven we heard,*
> *when we were with him in the holy mount.*
> We have also a more sure word of prophecy;
> *whereunto ye do well that ye take heed, as unto a light*
> *that shineth in a dark place, until the day dawn, and the*
> *day star arise in your hearts. . . .* [22]

In discussing this passage of scripture, the Prophet Joseph Smith said:

> *. . .now wherein could they have a more sure word of*
> *prophecy than to hear the voice of God saying, This is my*
> *beloved Son.*
> *Now for the secret and grand key.* Though they
> might hear the voice of God and know that Jesus was the
> Son of God, this would be no evidence that their election
> and calling was made sure, *that they had part with Christ,*
> *and were joint heirs with Him.* They then would want
> that more sure word of prophecy, *that they were sealed in*
> *the heavens and had the promise of eternal life in the*
> *kingdom of God. . . .* [23]

Herein lies an important principle: though a man may entertain angels, the son, or even the Father Himself, he still has no guarantee of eternal life unless he has received the more sure word of prophecy.

Finally, we are informed that the Hebrew Church "came into an innumerable company of angels, unto God the Father of all, and to Jesus Christ the Mediator of the new covenant." [24]

BLESSINGS OF THE SECOND COMFORTER ENJOYED IN THE AMERICAS.

That the Nephite people enjoyed the same blessings as the Hebrew Church is very evident from the *Book of Mormon.* Nephi, the son of Lehi, wrote of himself and his brother Jacob:

> *And now I, Nephi, write more of the words of
> Isaiah, for my soul delighteth in his words. For I will liken
> his words unto my people, and I will send them forth unto
> all my children, for* he verily saw my Redeemer, even as I
> have seen him.
>   *And my brother, Jacob, also has seen him as I have
> seen him. . . .* [25]

The Brother of Jared exercised faith of such magnitude that
he could not be kept from beholding within the veil.

> *. . .behold, the Lord showed himself unto him, and said:
> Because thou knowest these things ye are redeemed from
> the fall; therefore ye are brought back into my presence;
> therefore* I show myself unto you. [26]

Finally, one of the most beautiful accounts and descriptions
of the Second Comforter is given to us by Moroni, the son of
Mormon:

> *And now I, Moroni, bid farewell unto the Gentiles,
> yea, and also unto my brethren whom I love, until we
> shall meet before the judgement-seat of Christ, where all
> men shall know that my garments are not spotted with
> your blood.*
>   And then shall ye know that I have seen Jesus, and
> that he hath talked with me face to face, *and that he told
> me in plain humility, even as a man telleth another in
> mine own language, concerning these things. . . .* [27]

DOCTRINE OF SEALING
A PART OF THE RESTORED CHURCH.

The blessing of being sealed unto eternal life is as vital a
part of the Dispensation of the Fulness of Times as any other
gospel dispensation. In a communication to William Clayton
dated May 16, 1843, the Modern Seer said:

> *Your life is hid with Christ in God, and so are many others. Nothing but the unpardonable sin can prevent you from inheriting eternal life, for* you are sealed up by the power of the Priesthood unto eternal life, *having taken the step necessary for that purpose.* [28]

That the power to seal up unto eternal life is inherent in the priesthood, and that the early Elders *did* utilize that power is evident from the following extract from the journal of Orson Pratt. Orson wrote of his work with Lyman Johnson in August of 1833 as follows:

> *The 26th, in the forenoon the Church at Charleston, Vt., with some other brethren from other towns, met together and called upon the Lord; and* the Lord heard their prayers and moved upon his servant Lyman by the power of the Holy Ghost to seal them up unto eternal life. *And after this the brethren arose one by one and said that they knew that their names were sealed in the Lamb's Book of Life, and they all did bear this glorious testimony save two or three.* [29]

We will consider one final account of persons being sealed unto eternal life in the history of the restored Church. This last account is a beautiful and vivid description, as told by Sister Mary Elizabeth Rollins Lightner, a woman who later became one of the Prophet Joseph's wives. Sister Lightner was at the time of this communication 87 years old:

> *I joined the Church in the year 1830, in Kirtland, Ohio, just six months after it was first organized. I was then twelve years old.*
>
> *The Smith family came to Kirtland early in the Spring of 1831. After they were settled in their house, mother and I went to see them. We had heard so much about the Golden Bible, as it was then called, that we were very anxious to hear more. The whole Smith family,*

excepting Joseph was there. As we stood talking to them, Brother Joseph and Martin Harris came in with two or three others. When the greetings were over, Brother Joseph looked around very solemnly (it was the first time some of them had ever seen him) and said, "There are enough here to hold a little meeting."

A board was put across two chairs to make seats. Martin Harris sat on a little box at Joseph's feet. They sang and prayed, then Joseph got up to speak. He began very solemnly and very earnestly; all at once his countenance changed and he stood mute. He turned so white, he seemed perfectly transparent. Those who looked at him that night said he looked like he had a search light within him. I never saw anything like it on earth. I could not take my eyes away from him, I remember I thought we could almost see the cheek bones through the flesh of his face. I shall remember him as he looked then as long as I live.

He stood some moments looking over the congregation, as if to pierce each heart then said, "Do you know who has been in your midst this night?" One of the Smiths said, "An angel of the Lord." Martin Harris said, "It was our Lord and Savior, Jesus Christ."

Joseph put his hand down on Martin's head and said, "The Spirit of God revealed that to thee. Yes, brothers and sisters, the Savior has been in your midst this night, and I want you all to remember it. *There is a veil over your eyes, for you could not endure to look upon him. You must be fed with milk, not with strong meat. I want you all to remember this as if it were the last thing that escapes my lips.* He has given you all to me, and commanded me to seal you up to Everlasting Life, *that where he is there you may be also. And if your are tempted of Satan say, 'Get behind me Satan, for my salvation is secure.' "* Then he knelt down and prayed. *And such a prayer, I never heard before or since. We all felt that he was talking to the Lord and the Spirit of the Lord rested down on the congregation.* [30]

SUMMARY

As a man continues to hunger and thirst after righteousness, he eventually receives the glorious word, "Son, thou shalt be exalted," and thus receives the assurance of eternal life. This is the more sure word of prophecy, and comes by revelation and through the proper priesthood channels. A person with this assurance has thus met the mortal challenge, and his calling and election is made sure. That is, the blessings and positions of trust that he was called and elected to receive in the pre-mortal existence are realized on earth. He then is entitled, if the Lord so wills it, to entertain Celestial beings, including the Father and Son, the spirits of just men made perfect, an innumerable company of angels, and the General Assembly and Church of the Firstborn. Many in the Church are of the mistaken notion that the power to seal unto eternal life was restored in 1836 by Elijah, and thus that no one was sealed before that time. However, the scriptures teach us that this power was obtained at the time Peter, James, and John restored the Melchizedek Priesthood in 1829. It is clear from numerous accounts that many were so sealed as early as 1831.

CHAPTER 3
—FOOTNOTES—

1. TPJS, p. 150
2. D&C 14:7
3. Bruce R. McConkie, *Mormon Doctrine*, Bookcraft, 1966, pp. 361-362.
4. TPJS, p. 149
5. *Ibid.*, p. 150
6. D&C 76:53
7. TPJS, pp. 189, 365; Alma 13
8. TPJS, p. 149
9. D&C 131:5
10. *Ibid.*, 132:26-27
11. Matthew 12:31; Hebrews 6:4-6; D&C 76:31-35
12. TPJS, pp. 150-151
13. D&C 88:3-4
14. Solomon P. Kimball, *Life of David P. Kimball*, pp. 125-127.
15. DHC 1:283; D&C 76:67
16. TPJS, p. 325
17. D&C 76:67
18. *Ibid.*, 68:8, 12
19. Ephesians 1:13-14
20. TPJS, p. 149
21. 2 Peter 1:8-11
22. *Ibid.*, 1:16-19
23. TPJS, p. 298
24. *Ibid.*, p. 325
25. 2 Nephi 11:2-3
26. Ether 3:13
27. *Ibid.*, 12:38-39
28. DHC 5:391
29. *Journal of Orson Pratt,* under date of August 26, 1833.
30. *Young Woman's Journal*, Vol. 16, pp. 556-557 (December, 1905).

CHAPTER 4

ZION: THE ECONOMIC AND SOCIAL ORDERS

THE LORD'S LAW OF ECONOMICS

The powers of the Holy Ghost are of an enlivening and enlightening nature. The Spirit of God, because of its purging and cleansing actions, causes vital changes in the nature of its recipients. This divine influence fills one with a heavenly love, such that the person under its influence loves and forgives every soul. This Spirit prompts man to deal justly and fairly with his fellow beings,[1] creating a society of Saints who love their neighbors as themselves. Having this quality of the Spirit, people automatically begin to enter into free and open unions with one another, and likewise into covenant relationships, the highest form of human interaction. A natural consequence of this is the establishment of the Law of Consecration and Stewardship, a divine system of economics and property management. And thus after a people have become one in all things they maintain a society which is composed of all those things which uplift both mind and body, and lead to God.

CONSECRATION.

The Law of Consecration and Stewardship was first given by revelation to Joseph Smith on February 9, 1831. The Lord has referred to this law as the "law of the celestial kingdom," and has assured the Saints that Zion can only be built when the principles of this order are in effect. [2]   In order to participate in the Law of Consecration, one must be regenerated by the powers of the Holy Spirit, in order that he will truly love and esteem his brother as himself. The basis of this law is that the earth is the Lord's and the fulness thereof; [3]   all property belongs to Christ. Those endowed in the House of the Lord make solemn covenant to consecrate all they possess to the Church and Kingdom of God on earth.

The act of consecration is to the Lord through the Bishop of the Church. In a special letter to Bishop Edward Partridge, the Prophet explained that the Church is ". . . bound by the law of the Lord to give a *deed*, securing to him who receives inheritances, his inheritance for an everlasting inheritance, or in other words to be his individual property, his private stewardship. . . ." [4]   By mutual consent of the individual and the Bishop, a decision is reached as to how much and what type of property is deeded back to the person.

The matter of consecration must be done by the mutual consent of both parties; for to give the Bishop power to say how much every man shall have, and he be obliged to comply with the Bishop's judgement, is giving to the Bishop more power than a king has; and, upon the other hand, to let every man say how much he needs and the Bishop be obliged to comply with his judgement, is to throw Zion into confusion and make a slave of the Bishop. The fact is, there must be a balance or equilibrium of power, between the Bishop and the people; and thus harmony and good-will may be preserved among you. . . . But in the case the two parties cannot come to a mutual agreement, the Bishop is to have nothing to do about receiving such consecrations; and the case must be laid before a council of twelve high priests, the Bishop not being one of the council, but he is to lay the case before them. [5]

This portion of property deeded back to the individual is dependent upon family, circumstances, just wants, needs, and ability to manage the property. [6] Though one's family size or circumstance might necessitate his receiving a larger stewardship than another, yet all are on the same general standard of living, for it is not the will of the Lord ". . . that one man should possess that which is above another." [7]

STEWARDSHIP.

Having consecrated all to the Lord and entered into this holy order, a man may thus become an *heir* of God [8] and a joint heir unto Christ. Joseph Smith explained that ". . . a man is bound by the law of the Church, to consecrate to the Bishop, before he can be considered a legal heir to the kingdom of Zion; and this, too, without constraint; and unless he does this, he cannot be acknowledged before the Lord on the Church book." [9] In this order, the participant need not feel uncomfortable in asking for financial assistance, for as an heir all that the Father has is available for us. As heirs, the Saints have the right to act as *stewards* over the Lord's property which has been deeded back to them.

> *And it shall come to pass, that after they are laid before the bishop of my church, and after that he has received these testimonies concerning the consecration of the properties of my church,* . . . every man shall be made accountable unto me, a steward over his own property, or that which he has received by consecration, *as much as is sufficient for himself and family.* [10]

Each steward manages his stewardship in the most effective way, to improve upon and expand his talents (financial holdings). Through the eternal principle of competition, the individual makes his goods and services [11] available on the open market; this helps to upgrade the quality of the goods and services produced. Leonard J. Arrington explained the mechanics of this system in early Zion:

> *Each member was free to work as he pleased within the limitations of his stewardship. The profit system, the forces of supply and demand, and the price system presumably would continue to allocate resources, guide production decisions, and distribute primary or earned income. Some of the institutions of capitalism were thus retained and a considerable amount of economic freedom was permitted. Above all, there was to be no communism of goods. While "God's chosen" were counseled to "live together in love," they were also admonished to "pay for that which thou shalt receive of thy brother."* [12]

THE STOREHOUSE.

All funds obtained above and beyond the expenses necessary to support the family are turned over to the Bishop for deposit in the *storehouse*, the center of economic interests in the community.[13] This is one means by which surplus is built up in the storehouse (i.e., by surplus production). Another means is through surplus consecrations.[14] Surplus in the storehouse is used for community needs,[15] for individuals who desire to expand their stewardships,[16] and for the creation of new stewardships.[17] Each steward has the right to draw upon the storehouse to improve upon or expand his stewardship.

> *Therefore, I give unto you this commandment, that ye bind yourselves by this covenant, and it shall be done according to the laws of the Lord.*
> *Behold, here is wisdom also in me for your good.*
> And you are to be equal, or in other words, you are to have equal claims on the properties, for the benefit of managing the concerns of your stewardships, every man according to his wants and his needs, inasmuch as his wants are just. . . . [18]

MANAGEMENT OF STEWARDSHIPS.

The Lord explained that each steward is to be wise in the management of his stewardship, in order to improve upon that which he has been given. To insure that all are valiant in the managing process, a revelation explained that "... it is required of the Lord, at the hand of every steward, to render an account of his stewardship, both in time and in eternity."[19] To render an account of the stewardship in time probably has reference to the system of audit, in which the Bishop is apprised as to the productivity of the steward.[20] This audit does not extend to the management of family expenditures, for these are private matters.[21] To render an account in eternity undoubtedly refers to the steward's responsibility to God concerning management of the stewardship.[22] Any member of the Church leaving the order because of apostasy and ultimate excommunication had no claim on the surplus he had consecrated, but could retain his stewardship. Thus the Lord stated that "he that sinneth and repenteth not shall be cast out, and shall not receive again that which he has consecrated unto me...."[23] Speaking of the individual in sin, Joseph Smith said:

> ...if he is found a transgressor and should be cut off, out of the Church, his inheritance is his still, and he is delivered over to the buffetings of Satan till the day of redemption. But the property which he consecrated to the poor, for their benefit and inheritance and stewardship (i.e., his surplus), he cannot obtain again by the law of the Lord. Thus you see the propriety of this law, that rich men cannot have power to disinherit the poor by obtaining again that which they have consecrated....[24]

THE UNITED ORDER.

By revelation the Lord gave instructions to the Prophet Joseph to organize the United Order. The United Order was to serve to coordinate the various *communities* within the Lord's system; basically, it would serve to maintain oneness and equality among communities as the Law of Consecration had done with individuals within a community. The United Order also served to coordinate the various corporative stewardships that had been established within the system, such as the United Firm[25] and the Literary Firm.[26]

VALUE OF THE LORD'S PROGRAM.

The advantages of the Lord's Law of Economics are many. First of all, oneness and equality are established and maintained by and through the powers of the Holy Spirit. The request of the Lord to "be one" is thus granted.[27]   Second, the Lord's system makes possible the two extremes of mature individualism and social union. These are both made possible by the active powers of the Spirit as they act on man to (1) bring him to a point of personal sanctification, and (2) bring righteous men into a loyal union with one another. Third, this divine system combines the advantages of both the Open and Closed societies, while avoiding the disadvantages of each. Thus freedom, security, initiative, and a feeling of community are maintained, while coercion, chaos, and loneliness are done away. Fourth, unlimited property-getting is done away, as well as the great propertyless group who work for others.[28]   Finally, this type of society is capable of standing independent of the entire world. The Prophet Joseph Smith said: "It was my endeavor to so organize the church, that the brethren might eventually be independent of every incumbrance beneath the celestial kingdom, by bonds and covenants of mutual friendship, and mutual love."[29]

THE SOCIAL ORDER IN ZION

The society of Zion is composed of all things which uplift both mind and body, and thus lead to God. Regarding the social aspects of Zion, the Latter-day Saints hold to the philosophy that there ". . . is no true enjoyment in life—nothing that can be a blessing to an individual or to a community, but what is ordained of God to bless his people."[30] In Zion, recreational activities serve many functions. President Brigham Young taught that these types of activities act literally to re-create the mind and body. He said:

> We are now enjoying our pastimes. We often meet together and worship the Lord by singing, praying, and preaching, fasting, and communing with each other in the Sacrament of the Lord's Supper. Now we are met in the capacity of a social community—for what? That our minds may rest, and our bodies receive that recreation which is proper and necessary to keep up an equilibrium to promote healthy action in the whole system.
>
> Let our minds sing for joy, and let life diffuse itself into every avenue of the body; for the object of our meeting is for its exercise, for its good.[31]

President Young further said concerning the attitude the Saints must have in recreational activities:

> Those that have kept the covenants and served their God, if they wish to exercise themselves in any way to rest their minds and tire their bodies, go and enjoy yourselves in the dance, and let God be in all your thoughts in this as in all things, and he will bless you.[32]

CULTURAL ACTIVITIES IN EARLY ZION.

The cultural aspects of the cities of Zion in the history of the Church provided a healthy and wholesome atmosphere for the Saints to raise up a righteous and intelligent posterity. Debates were a common occurrence in early Church history, and for some time were held weekly.[33] These debates were entered into by men and women ". . . for the purpose of eliciting truth, acquiring

knowledge, and improving public speaking.'' [34] Joseph
Smith reported the following concerning the evening of
December 12, 1835:

> *In the evening attended a debate at Brother William
> Smith's on the following question—Was it necessary for
> God to reveal Himself to mankind in order for their
> happiness? I was on the affirmative, and the last to speak
> on that side of the question.*[35]

Also very prevalent in early Mormon society were
demonstrations of other artistic abilities through pain-
tings,[36] lyceums,[37] museums,[38] and drama.[39] At the
University of the City of Nauvoo, the Music Department
often entertained audiences in musical lyseums.[40] The
philosophy of the Latter-day Saints toward music is worth
considering in more detail at this point. President Brigham
Young reported:

> *There is no music in hell, for* all good music belongs
> to heaven. *Sweet harmonious sounds give exquisite joy to
> human beings capable of appreciating music. I delight in
> hearing harmonious tunes made by the human voice, by
> musical instruments, and by both combined. Every sweet
> musical sound that can be made belongs to the Saints and
> is for the Saints.*[41]

Joseph Young spoke of the Prophet Joseph Smith and his
(the Prophet's) feelings toward vocal music:

> *He recommended the Saints to cultivate as high a state of
> perfection in their musical harmonies as the standard of
> the faith which he had brought was superior to sectarian
> religion. To obtain this, he gave them to understand that
> the refinement of singing would depend on the attainment
> of the Holy Spirit. . . . When these graces and refinements
> and all the kindred attractions are obtained that
> characterized the ancient Zion of Enoch, then the Zion of*

*the last days will become beautiful, she will be hailed by
the Saints from the four winds, who will gather to Zion
with songs of everlasting joy.*[42]

MARRIAGE AS A SOCIAL INSTITUTION.

The philosophy of the Latter-day Saints toward
marriage is a lofty one, emphasizing the eternal fact that
"marriage is ordained of God."[43] The New and
Everlasting Covenant of Marriage, entered into only in the
Temples of God, is the basis of the Divine Patriarchal
Order. In discussing the all-encompassing nature of this
holy order, President Brigham Young said:

> ...*the whole subject of the marriage relation is not in my
> reach, nor in any other man's reach on this earth. It is
> without beginning of days or end of years: it is a hard
> matter to reach. We can tell some things with regard to
> it: it lays the foundation for worlds, for angels, and for
> the Gods; for intelligent beings to be crowned with glory,
> immortality, and eternal lives. In fact, it is the thread
> which runs from the beginning to the end of the holy
> Gospel of Salvation—of the Gospel of the Son of God; it is
> from eternity to eternity.*[44]

Within this sacred order of the marriage relation is the
equally eternal principle of Plurality of Wives.[45] This
divine law has been given to the Saints of God in generations
past in order to raise up seed unto Christ. It is a sacred order,
and thus one to be practiced *only when the Lord com-
mands;* otherwise, the participant is guilty of committing
adultery.[46] We learn from the Prophets that Adam, for
example, lived the higher law of plural marriage, having
more than one wife.[47] Other great men through the
centuries such as Abraham, Isaac, Jacob, Moses, David,
Solomon, and Joseph Smith received the same commandment to take more than one wife.[48] This aspect of the
New Everlasting Covenant is one that must eventually be

practiced by every man before he can hope to gain the fulness of the Father's glory.[49]   William Clayton said:

> *From him (Joseph Smith) I learned that the doctrine of plural and celestial marriage is the most holy and important doctrine ever revealed to man on the earth and that* without obedience to that principle no man can ever attain to the fulness of exaltation in celestial glory.[50]

President Brigham Young said simply, "The only men who become Gods, even the sons of God, are those who enter polygamy."[51]

The practical benefits of plural marriage are many. First, much of the promiscuous sexual activity of the present day is done away, inasmuch as (1) husbands are deprived of an excuse for extramarital relations, and (2) unmarried women are removed from the prey of perverse men. In this sense, polygamy aims at social reform. Second, healthy tabernacles are provided in which pure spirits may dwell, and the Saints are able to "raise up seed unto Christ." Third, through living this sacred law, men and women are renewed by the powers of the Spirit. Elder Heber C. Kimball spoke of this advantage to the participants of polygamy:

> *I would not be afraid to promise a man who is sixty years of age, if he will take the counsel of brother Brigham and his brethren, that* he will renew his age. *I have noticed that a man that has but one wife, and is inclined to that doctrine, soon begins to wither and dry up, while a man who goes into plurality looks fresh, young and sprightly. Why is this? Because God loves that man, and because he honors his work and word. Some of you may not believe this; but I not only believe it—I also know it.*[52]

And thus we see that Zion will give the answers to the world's problems in all aspects of human existence.

EDUCATION IN EARLY ZION.

President Brigham Young made it clear that "Not only does the religion of Jesus Christ make the people acquainted with the things of God,. . . but it holds out every encouragement and inducement, for them to increase in knowledge and intelligence, in every branch of mechanism. . . ."[53] Joseph Smith felt the need of education for all, and hence organized grammar schools, common schools, and high schools among the Saints.[54] Concerning the Kirtland School, Elder William E. McLellin wrote:

> The school has been conducted under the immediate care and inspection of Joseph Smith, Jun., Frederick G. Williams, Sidney Rigdon, and Oliver Cowdery, trustees. . . . Since the year 1827, I have taught school in five different states, and visited many schools in which I was not engaged as teacher; in none, I can say with certainty, I have seen students make more rapid progress than in this.[55]

At the center of the school system in Nauvoo was the University of the City of Nauvoo, into which all educational pursuits were coordinated. The University was established as an institution of learning by the Nauvoo City Council for the ". . . teaching of the Arts, Sciences, and learned professions."[56] The institution was under the direction of a Board of Trustees, consisting of a Chancellor, Registrar, and twenty-three regents.[57] In a letter to the Saints scattered abroad, the First Presidency of the Church wrote the following in January of 1841:

> The "University of the City of Nauvoo" will enable us to teach our children wisdom, to instruct them in all the knowledge and learning, in the arts, sciences, and learned professions. We hope to make this institution one

*of the great lights of the world, and by and through it to
diffuse that kind of knowledge which will be of practicable
utility, and for the public good, and also for private and
individual happiness.*[58]

For some years the School of the Prophets stood at the
apex of Zion's system of learning. Joseph Smith received
instructions in December of 1832 to organize a school of
priesthood holders, and to teach them the doctrines of the
Kingdom.[59]   These men enjoyed the higher blessings of the
Spirit, having received the promise of eternal life.[60]   This
select group learned the things of God by the outpouring of
the Spirit, as indicated in the following statement by Joseph
Smith:

*Great and glorious were the divine manifestations of the
Holy Spirit. Praises were sung to God and the Lamb;
speaking and praying, all in tongues, occupied the
conference until a late hour at night, so rejoiced were we
at the return of these long absent blessings.*[61]

THE PHILOSOPHY OF EDUCATION IN ZION.

The philosophy of education in the Society of Zion rests
upon the basic principle that revelation is the most effective
means of obtaining knowledge. This principle is best
demonstrated by the statement of the Lord in 1832:

*And as all have not faith, seek ye diligently and teach
one another words of wisdom; yea, seek ye out of the best
books words of wisdom; seek learning, even by study and
also by faith.*[62]

The Lord here states that those who do not have faith
(sufficient to receive knowledge by revelation) should seek
knowledge by study and use of the human intellect. But for
those who *do* have faith, revelation is the pattern of growing
in intelligence. Sidney Rigdon expressed this philosophy at

the dedicatory services of the cornerstone of the Far West Temple:

> *One part of the House shall be set apart for a place to worship where* we shall invoke our God for revelations when we have gone as far as human skill can carry us. *That by revelations, visions, etc., we may fill the vacuum still left after science and philosophy have done all they can, so that we may have that understanding and wisdom which brings salvation and that knowledge which is unto eternal life.*
> ...when science fails, revelation supplies its place, *and unfolds the secrets and mysteries of the unseen world, leads the mind into knowledge of the future existence of man, makes it acquainted with angels, principalities, and powers, in the eternal worlds....*[63]

The system of education in Zion aims at a synthesis of knowledge and an integration of truth, so that all truth may be circumscribed into one great whole. Brigham Young stated:

> *When we have faith to understand that he must dictate, and that we must be perfectly submissive to him, then we shall begin to rapidly collect the intelligence that is bestowed upon nations, for all this intelligence belongs to Zion.* All the knowledge, wisdom, power, and glory that have been bestowed upon the nations of the earth, from the days of Adam till now, must be gathered home to Zion.[64]

It is thus the ultimate purpose and design of the educational system of Zion to bring the Saints along the long continuum of faith to that point where they qualify for the type of divine teaching undertaken in the School of the Prophets.

SUMMARY

As the Holy Spirit works on the minds and hearts of men, noticeable changes are evident. The regenerated man feels the need to enter into covenant relationships and to consecrate all to the Lord through the Church program. The Law of Consecration and Stewardship, as it is organized within the United Order, makes possible the total unity and equality that could only exist among a people that are pure in heart. Although there is a union of property, each participant has many private rights, some of which include:

1.   The right to be a steward over property, or the right to responsibility.[65]
2.   The right to determine, with the Bishop, the size and type of stewardship.[66]
3.   The right to draw upon the storehouse.[67]
4.   The right of a steward's widow and children to be provided for from the surplus of the storehouse.[68]
5.   The right of his children to receive stewardships from the storehouse upon beginning their own families.[69]

Recreational and cultural activities are and will continue to be a vital part of the society of the people of God; it is through these types of activities that the Saints become "whole" in their approach to life. Marriage under the New and Everlasting Covenant is viewed by Latter-day Saints as honorable and noble, and the only means by which the Divine Patriarchal Order is to be perfected. The Latter-day Saints view revelation as the prime source of knowledge, and seek to grow in faith to the point where all things are learned in this way.

CHAPTER 4
—FOOTNOTES—

1. D&C 11:12; 82:19
2. D&C 105:1-5
3. Psalms 24:1; compare D&C 38:17-18; 104:54-55
4. Joseph Smith, Jr., to Edward Partridge, May 2, 1833, as cited in O.F. Whitney, ''The Aaronic Priesthood,'' *The Contributor*, VI (October, 1884), p. 7.
5. TPJS, p. 23; see also D&C 51:4
6. D&C 51:3
7. *Ibid.,* 49:20
8. *Ibid.,* 70:8
9. TPJS, p. 23
10. D&C 42:32; see also *Ibid.,* 104:13, 56
11. See, for example, D&C 70:12 and 72:14. Not all will have stewardships over temporal matters.
12. Leonard J. Arrington, ''Early Mormon Communitarianism: The Law of Consecration and Stewardship,'' *Western Humanities Review,* VII (Autumn, 1953), p. 344. See also Joseph A. Geddes, *The United Order Among the Mormons,* Deseret News Press, Salt Lake City, 1924, pp. 32, 163-164. Compare D&C 42:45-54.
13. D&C 42:33-35; 51:13; 70:7
14. *Ibid.,* 42:33
15. *Ibid.,* 42:34-35
16. *Ibid.,* 104:68-77
17. *Ibid.,* 83:5
18. *Ibid.,* 82:15-17
19. *Ibid.,* 72:3
20. *Ibid.,* 72
21. See Orson Pratt in JD 17:32-33
22. See D&C 42:32; *Ibid.,* 51:19; *Ibid.,* 78:22
23. *Evening and Morning Star* (Independence, Missouri), I (July 1832), p. 1.
24. Joseph Smith, Jr., to Edward Partridge, May 2, 1833, as cited in O.F. Whitney, ''The Aaronic Priesthood,'' *The Contributor,* VI (October 1884), p. 7. Note: It is very interesting that the person in sin receives the same punishment (turned over to the buffetings of Satan) as one sealed unto eternal life who commits wilful sin (see D&C 132:26). This adds some credence to the possibility that those participants in the Law of Consecration and Stewardship were Saints who were *truly* heirs of God, having received the promise of eternal life. On one occasion the Lord spoke to the directors of the United Order and referred to them as the ''Church of the Firstborn,'' which organization no one enters unless he has received the assurance of eternal life. See D&C 78.
25. DHC 1:270
26. *Ibid.,* 2:273, 482; D&C 70
27. D&C 38:27
28. See Joseph A. Geddes, *The United Order Among the Mormons,* Salt Lake City, Deseret News Press, 1924, p. 32.

29. DHC 1:269; compare D&C 78:14-15
30. See Brigham Young in JD 6:143
31. *Ibid.*, 1:29
32. *Ibid.*, 1:30
33. See DHC 2:317, 330; *Ibid.*, 4:514; see also *Excerpts from the Diary of Wandle Mace,* p. 23.
34. DHC 4:514
35. *Ibid.*, 2:330
36. *Ibid.*, 6:471
37. See *Diary of Wandle Mace,* p. 83
38. *Times and Seasons,* Vol. 4, pp. 201-203
39. DHC 6:349-350
40. *Times and Seasons,* Vol. 3, p. 666
41. JD 9:244
42. Joseph Young, "Vocal Music," in *History of the Organization of the Seventies,* Deseret News Steam Printing Establishment, 1878, pp. 14-15.
43. D&C 49:15
44. JD 2:90
45. D&C 132
46. Jacob 2:23-30
47. Brigham Young, JD 1:50-51; see also *Journal of Wilford Woodruff* under date of April 9, 1852.
48. D&C 132:1, 37-38
49. See *Journal History* (October 9, 1869), pp. 6-7; compare D&C 132:4, 6, 33
50. *Historical Record* 6:226
51. JD 11:26; *Ibid.,* 20:28; *Millennial Star* 5:15
52. JD 5:22
53. JD 13:147
54. DHC 1:276
55. *Ibid.,* 2:200
56. *Ibid.,* 4:243
57. *Ibid.,* 4:244
58. *Ibid.,* 4:269
59. D&C 88:77, 118
60. *Ibid.,* 88:3-5, 138; DHC 1:323
61. DHC 1:322-323
62. D&C 88:118
63. Sidney Rigdon, Remarks at the Dedicatory Services of the Cornerstone at the Far West Temple. Far West, Missouri, July 4, 1832. For more on the principle of learning by faith, see B.H. Roberts, *Discourses of B.H. Roberts,* pp. 25-26 (Quoted by Roy W. Doxey, "Great Truths; The School of the Prophets," *The Relief Society Magazine* (November 1965), p. 131.
64. JD 8:278
65. D&C 42:32; *Ibid.,* 104:13, 56; *Ibid.,* 70:12
66. TPJS, p. 23; D&C 42:32; D&C 51:3-4
67. D&C 82:15-17; *Ibid.,* 104:72-73
68. *Ibid.,* 42:33-34; *Ibid.,* 83:2
69. *Ibid.,* 82:17-18; *Ibid.,* 83:5

CHAPTER 5

THE GOVERNMENT OF GOD

The Prophet Joseph envisioned a Kingdom[1] which provided for the spiritual, socio-economic, and political needs of man. The establishment of the political program of the Lord is in direct fulfillment of the prophecy of Daniel:

> *And in the days of these kings shall the God of heaven set up a kingdom, which shall never be destroyed: and the kingdom shall not be left to other people, but it shall break in pieces and consume all these kingdoms, and it shall stand for ever.*[2]

President Brigham Young thus informed us that "This kingdom is the kingdom that Daniel spoke of, which was to be set up in the last days; it is the kingdom that is not to be given to another people; it is the kingdom that is to be held by the servants of God, to rule the nations of the earth. . . ."[3] Similarly, Elder Orson Pratt declared that "There is now organized on the earth a government which will never be broken as former governments have been. This will stand forever."[4]

THE GOVERNMENT OF GOD ORGANIZED

The nucleus[5] of the political program of God was established on March 11, 1844 by the Prophet Joseph

Smith. A group of men were organized into a "special council" to watch over and care for the Saints in Illinois and to investigate the possibility of a place of refuge in the West:

> *Present—Joseph Smith, Hyrum Smith, Brigham Young, Heber C. Kimball, Willard Richards, Parley P. Pratt, Orson Pratt, John Taylor, George A. Smith, William W. Phelps, John M. Bernhiesel, Lucien Woodworth, George Miller, Alexander Badlam, Peter Haws, Erastus Snow, Reynolds Cahoon, Amos Fielding, Alpheus Cutler, Levi Richards, Newel K. Whitney, Lorenzo D. Wasson, and William Clayton,* whom I organized into a special council *to take into consideration. . . the best policy for this people to adopt to obtain their rights from the nation and insure protection for themselves and children; and to secure a resting place in the mountains, or some uninhabited region. . . .*[6]

The official title of this body was given by revelation to be "The Kingdom of God and His laws with the keys and powers thereof and judgement in the hands of His servants."[7] There is some indication that Joseph received a revelation to organize this body as early as April 7, 1842.[8] The fact that the Prophet did wait until March of 1844 indicates the concern of the Modern Seer to avoid any Gentile claims of disloyalty or tyranny.[9] This special council became known by other titles, such as the "General Council,"[10] the "Council of the Kingdom,"[11] and the "Living Constitution."[12] Because the number of men in this body remained at about fifty for some time,[13] it was quite often referred to as the "Council of Fifty."[14] Though the members of the Quorum of the Twelve were all members of the General Council, yet it is not correct to assume that the Council was a priesthood or ecclesiastical organization. Benjamin F. Johnson thus reported that the Council consisted of "a select circle of the Prophet's most trusted friends, including the twelve but not all the con-

stituted authorities of the Church.'"[15]   At the death of the
Prophet Joseph, Alexander Badlam and Bishop George
Miller suggested that the General Council meet to
reorganize the Presidency of the Church. They were told
that

> ...*the Council of Fifty was not a church organization,
> but was composed of members irrespective of their
> religious faith, and organized for the purpose of con-
> sulting on the best manner of obtaining redress of
> grievances from our enemies, and to devise means to find
> and locate in some place where we could live in peace;
> and that* the organization of the church belonged to the
> priesthood alone.[16]

There is some evidence to indicate that Colonel Thomas L.
Kane and Daniel H. Wells, both non-members in the pre-
exodus period, were closely involved with (and probably
members of) the Council of Fifty.[17]   John D. Lee further
explained the relationship between this Council and the
Priesthood when he stated that "This council alluded to is
the Municipal department of the Kingdom of God set up on
the Earth, from which all law eminates, for the rule,
government and control of all Nations, Kingdoms and
Tongues and People under the whole Heavens but not to
control the Priesthood, but to council, deliberate and plan
for the general good and upbuilding of the Kingdom of God
on the Earth.[18]   This body of men, referred to as "the
highest court on earth,"[19]   dealt not only with political
matters of the Kingdom, but were also involved with many
other aspects of society. Some of the many involvements
included:[20]

1. Preparation for the exodus to the West.
2. Settling the Saints in the Great Basin.
3. Distribution of land.
4. Determination of water rights.

5. Legislation of cattle-control laws.
6. Selection of cemetery plots.
7. Reorganization of the Nauvoo Legion.
8. Pronouncements of capital punishment for such crimes as murder or adultery.

We are to understand that this political body grew out of the Church, for only through the efforts of spiritual men could the Kingdom of God be established. President John Taylor explained:

> We talk sometimes about the church of God, and why? We talk about the kingdom of God and why? Because, before there could be a kingdom of God, there must be a church of God, and hence the first principles of the gospel were needed to be preached to all nations, as they were formerly when the Lord Jesus Christ and others made their appearance on the earth. And why so? Because of the impossibility of introducing the law of God among a people who would not be subject to and guided by the spirit of revelation. Here the world have generally made great mistakes upon these points. They have started various projects to try to unite and cement the people together without God; but they could not do it. [21]

The separation of Church and State is maintained under the Lord's program, in the sense that ecclesiastical and political roles are separate. Elder George Q. Cannon thus said: "We have been taught from the beginning this important principle, that the church of God is distinct from the kingdom of God. . . . In the midst of all of us who understand this matter there is a clear distinction between the church in its ecclesiastical capacity and that which may be termed the government of God in its political capacity." [22]

THE THEOCRATIC
SYSTEM OF GOVERNMENT

In a *theocracy*, the will of the Lord rules and reigns supreme. Thus Brigham Young declared that the theocracy is "the only true form of government on earth."[23]   Orson Pratt stated that "The kingdom of God. . . is the only legal government that can exist in any part of the universe. All other governments are illegal and unauthorized."[24]   Elder Pratt likewise stated that "There is a nucleus of a government formed since that of the United States, which is perfect in its nature. It is perfect, having emanated from a being who is perfect."[25]

The Latter-day Saints hold that the Constitution of the United States is a divine document, prepared by men who were raised up by God to do an important work.[26]   The Lord said in a revelation:

> *And that law of the land which is constitutional, supporting that principle of freedom in maintaining rights and privileges, belongs to all mankind, and is justifiable before me.*
> *Therefore, I, the Lord, justify you, and your brethren of my church, in befriending that law which is the constitutional law of the land;*
> *And as pertaining to the law of man, whatsoever is more or less than this, cometh of evil.*[27]

It is interesting that the Lord indicates that we are "justified" in befriending the U.S. Constitution. This is not fully understood until we realize that the Constitution, though perhaps the closest approximation to the will of the Almighty,[28] is actually a "stepping stone to a form of government infinitely greater and more perfect—a government founded upon divine laws, and officers appointed by the God of heaven."[29]   Orson Pratt discussed this matter as follows:

> *Why did not the Lord, at the time, introduce a perfect government—a theocracy? It was simply because the people were not prepared for it. . . . They were far from being prepared for the government of God, which is a government of union.*
>
> *But* will the government of the United States continue forever? No, it is not sufficiently perfect; *and notwithstanding it has been sanctioned by the Lord at a time when it was suited to the circumstances of the people, yet the day will come. . . when the United States government, and all others, will be uprooted, and the kingdoms of this world will be united in one, and the kingdom of our God will govern the whole earth. . . .* [30]

This principle is also evident in a statement by the Lord when He instructs us to ". . . be subject to the powers that be, until he reigns whose right it is to reign, and subdues all enemies under his feet." [31]

The structure of the theocratic government resembles closely the present republican form of government in the United States. Said Brigham Young:

> *. . .few if any understand what a theocratic government is. In every sense of the word,* it is a republican government, and differs but little in form from our National, State, and Territorial Governments; but its subjects will recognize the will and dictation of the Almighty. [32]

President Young referred to the theocracy on another occasion as a "Republican Democratic Government."[33] Thus the Government of God is to incorporate all of the righteous principles of republicanism (where good and honorable men represent the voice of the people), while also incorporating some of the principles of the democracy (where the people have a voice). Orson Pratt described the establishment of a theocracy as a situation in which

... .all the great and glorious principles incorporated in this great republic will be incorporated in the kingdom of God and be preserved. *I mean the principles of civil and religious liberty, especially, and all other good principles that are contained in that great instrument framed by our forefathers will be incorporated in the kingdom of God; and only in this manner can all that is good in this and in foreign governments be preserved.*[34]

OPERATIONS OF THE POLITICAL KINGDOM

The Government of God acts in and through the Holy Priesthood, the word of God being manifest through the living Prophet. President John Taylor explained:

The proper mode of government is this—God first speaks, and then the people have their action. *It is for them to say whether they will have his dictation or not. They are free: they are independent under God. . . .still we believe there is a correct order—some wisdom and knowledge somewhere that is superior to ours: that wisdom and knowledge proceeds from God through the medium of the Holy Priesthood. . . .* [35]

Elder George A. Smith expressed the feeling that "Our system should be a *Theo-Democracy*—the voice of the people consenting to the voice of God."[36] Joseph Smith said simply, "I go for a theo-democracy."[37] A more thorough description of the process of the theo-democracy or theocracy is given in the following statement from the *Millennial Star:*

At mass meetings, held in all the principal precincts, delegates are chosen by unanimous vote to meet in a convention, and select the names of individuals to fill the various vacant offices. In case of any dispute or dubiety on

*the mind of the convention, the Prophet of God, who
stands at the head of the Church, decides. He nominates,
the convention endorses, and the people accept the
nomination. . . . So in the legislature itself. . . . the word
of the Lord, through the head of the Church, guides,
counsels, and directs.*[38]

Elder Parley P. Pratt also made it clear that the voice of the
people "is rather a sanction, a strength and support to that
which God chooses. But they do not confer the authority in
the first place, nor can they take it away."[39]   President
Brigham Young spoke of the value of direct revelation in the
Government of God:

*Few, if any, understand what a theocratic government
is. . . .* its subjects will recognize the will and dictation of
the Almighty. *The kingdom of God circumscribes and
comprehends the municipal laws for the people in their
outward government, to which pertain the Gospel
covenants, by which the people can be saved; and these
covenants pertain to fellowship and faithfulness.*[40]

President Young said on another occasion:

What do I understand by a theocratic government?
One in which all laws are enacted and executed in
righteousness, and whose officers possess that power
which proceedeth from the Almighty. *That is the kind of
government I allude to when I speak of a theocratic
government, or the kingdom of God upon the earth. It is,
in short, the eternal powers of the Gods.* [41]

Inasmuch as the will of the Lord will be done on earth
among the people of God, and the Society of Zion will be
united in its political views, there will be no need for
political parties in government.[42]   In fact, President Young
declared that at that moment when political opposition is
permitted to enter into governmental institutions, the seeds
of error and corruption begin to grow.[43]

Since Zion will open its doors to the honorable and just men of the earth, there is no question that these honorable men will not only live under the protecting shield of Zion's walls, but will also take an active part in legislating and executing the Government of God. Brigham Young stated that ''a man may be a legislator in that body which will issue laws to sustain the inhabitants of the earth in their individual rights and still not belong to the Church of Jesus Christ at all.''[44] Elder George Q. Cannon commented:

> *Joseph Smith set the pattern; he taught the brethren who were with him better ideas; you well-informed Latter-day Saints know that there are two powers which God has restored in these the last days. One is the Church of God, and the other is the Kingdom of God.* A man may belong to the Kingdom of God and yet not be a member of the Church of God. *In the Kingdom of God, using it in the political sense, there may be heathens and Pagans and Mohammedans and Latter-day Saints and Presbyterians and Episcopalians and Catholics and men of every creed. Will they legislate for the Church of Jesus Christ alone? . . . No. Why? Because God is the Father of the Latter-day Saints as well as of every human being. . . .*[45]

Similarly, Elder Cannon said on a different occasion:

> *There may be men acting as officers in the Kingdom of God who will not be members of the Church of Jesus Christ of Latter-day Saints. On this point the Prophet Joseph gave particular instructions before his death, and gave an example, which he asked the younger elders who were present to always remember. It was to the effect that* men might be chosen to officiate as members of the Kingdom of God who had no standing in the Church of Jesus Christ of Latter-day Saints.[46]

THE KINGDOM OF GOD AS A REFUGE

As the nations and kingdoms of the world crumble to dust,[47] the Kingdom of God will stand tall as an ensign of unity and stability. As the glory of the Lord rests upon Zion, those who refuse to enter into war with one another will flee to the stronghold of the Government of God among the Saints.[48] President John Taylor commented on the state of things at that day and said that ". . .when the nations shall be convulsed, we may stand forth as saviours, and do that which will be best calculated to produce the well-being of the human family, . . .not only in a religious but in a political point of view."[49] President Taylor went on to say:

> *Now as to the great future what shall we say? Why, a little stone has been cut out of the mountains without hands, and this little stone is becoming a great nation, and it will eventually fill the whole earth. How will it fill it, religiously? Yes, and politically too, for it will have the rule, the power, the authority, the dominion in its own hands. This is the position we are destined to occupy. . . I expect one nation after another to rise against us until they will all be broken to pieces.*[50]

Thus all men of good will may enjoy the security and protection of the Government of God. President Brigham Young said:

> *"We offer you life; will you receive it?" "No," some will say. "Then you are at perfect liberty to choose death: the Lord does not, neither will we control you in the least in the exercise of your agency. We place the principles of life before you. Do as you please, and we will protect you in your rights, though you will learn that the system you have chosen to follow brings you to dissolution—to being resolved to native element."*[51]

It appears from the writings and discourses of the early brethren that those outside the Church will not be required to profess an active belief in Mormonism per se, but they will be required to bow the knee, confess that Jesus is the Christ and Lawgiver, and abide by moral and ethical principles. This is demonstrated in a Proclamation of the Twelve Apostles at the deaths of Joseph and Hyrum Smith:

> *The Kingdom of God consists in correct principles;*
> *and* it mattereth not what a man's religious faith is. . . if
> he will bow the knee and with his tongue confess that
> Jesus is the Christ, and will support good and wholesome
> laws *for the regulation of society. . . . but if he shall deny*
> *Jesus, if he shall curse God, if he shall indulge in*
> *debauchery and drunkeness, and crime; if he shall lie,*
> *and swear, and steal; if he shall take the name of the great*
> *God in vain, and commit all manners of abominations, he*
> *shall have no place in our midst. . . .*[52]

Brigham Young also made it clear that people coming to Zion for protection would not necessarily want to become a part of the Church organization:

> *If the Latter-day Saints think, when the Kingdom of*
> *God is established on the earth, that all the inhabitants of*
> *the earth will join the church called Latter-day Saints,*
> *they are egregiously mistaken.* I presume there will be as
> many sects and parties then as now. *Still, when the*
> *Kingdom of God triumphs, every knee shall bow and*
> *every tongue confess that Jesus is the Christ, to the glory*
> *of the Father. Even the Jews will do it then; but will the*
> *Jews and Gentiles be obliged to belong to the Church of*
> *Jesus Christ of Latter-day Saints? No; not by any means.*
> *Jesus said to his disciples, "In my Father's house are*
> *many mansions."*[53]

Zion's borders will expand eventually to cover the entire world. Brigham Young said that "Zion will extend, eventually to cover the entire world. There will be no nook or corner upon the earth but will be in Zion. It will all be in Zion."[54]

SUMMARY

The establishment of the Government of God is in direct fulfillment of the prophecy of Daniel. The Kingdom of God is that kingdom which will stand as the social and political systems of the world collapse. On March 11, 1844, the Prophet Joseph Smith organized the General Council, a body of men which served as the nucleus of the political kingdom. The early brethren of the Church taught that the political organ grows out of the Church, for only when a society is grounded in the powers of the Holy Spirit may the Government of God function. In the theocratic system of government, the will of the Lord rules in society. God's will is made known through the Living Prophet, and the people in society have the right to express their support or dissenting vote. Since Zion will open its doors to all the honorable and just of the earth, good men outside the Church will be sought for to work with the Priesthood in legislating and executing laws in the political system. The Kingdom of God will serve as a refuge for all of those who confess Christ as King, and agree to abide by moral and ethical standards. Zion will eventually expand to cover the entire earth, as "all nations flow unto it."

CHAPTER 5
—FOOTNOTES—

1. The expression "Kingdom of God" is often used to designate specifically the political program of the Lord or the Government of God, rather than the entire program (social, economic, spiritual). See, for example, JD 2:317; 6:25; 11:89-90; 15:44-45; 18:137; 20:204; 21:63-64; 23:177-178. See also JI, XXXI (1896), p. 140; John Taylor, *The Government of God,* London, LDS Book Depot, 1852; DHC 7:382.

2. Daniel 2:44

3. JD 17:156

4. *Ibid.,* 15:44-45

5. *Ibid.,* 3:71-72

6. DHC 6:260-261, 263-264; Ibid., 7:439

7. Minutes of the Council of Fifty, 1880 (Brigham Young University Library).

8. *Ibid.*

9. See Klaus Hansen, "The Political Kingdom of God as a Cause for Mormon-Gentile Conflict," *Brigham Young University Studies,* II (Spring-Summer 1960), pp. 241-260. See also Hansen's *Quest for Empire: The Political Kingdom of God and the Council of Fifty in Mormon History,* Michigan State University Press, 1970.

10. DHC 6:260-261, 274, 343, 356

11. George Miller, Sr. and George Miller, Jr., *A Mormon Bishop and His Son,* Fragments of a Diary Kept by George Miller, Sr., Bishop in the Mormon Church, and Some Records of Incidents in the Life of George Miller, Jr., Hunter and Pathfinder, ed. H. M. Mills (London, England; nd) p. 48

12. John D. Lee, *Mormonism Unveiled* (St. Louis, 1877), p. 173

13. "History of Brigham Young," *Millennial Star* 26:328-329

14. *Ibid.;* DHC 7:213

15. Benjamin F. Johnson to George S. Gibbs, April to October, 1903 (typed manuscript, Brigham Young University Library, p. 9).

16. DHC 7:213; *Millennial Star* 25:136

17. Cited by Klaus Hansen, *Quest for Empire,* Michigan State University Press, p. 62.

18. *A Mormon Chronicle: The Diaries of John D. Lee, 1848-1876,* ed. Robert Glass Cleland and Juanita Brooks (2 vols.; San Marino, Calif., 1955), I, p. 80.

19. James Holt, "The Reminiscences of James Holt. A Narrative of the Emmett Company," ed. Dale Morgan, *Utah Historical Quarterly,* XXV (1957), p. 107.

20. Each of the following are cited in Hansen's *Quest for Empire,* pp. 69-70, 80-81, 124-125.

21. JD 18:137; see also JD 1:173-174; 2:192-193, 317; 5:265; 10:240-241; 13:126; 21:65.

22. JI, XXXI (1896), p. 140; compare D & C 134:9

23. JD 7:8

24. Orson Pratt, *The Kingdom of God* (Liverpool, 1851). p. 1; see also JD 1:230
25. JD 3:71-72
26. D & C 101:80; see also JD 7:14; 20:204
27. D & C 98:5-7
28. Orson Pratt, JD 6:342
29. Orson Pratt, Ibid., 7:215. In a most interesting way, President Brigham Young drew a significant distinction between the Constitution and the "damned rascals who administer the government." See *Journal History*, September 8, 1851, p. 4.
30. JD 3:71-73; see also Orson Pratt, *The Seer* (1853), pp. 147-148.
31. D & C 58:22
32. JD 6:342
33. *Ibid.*, 7:8
34. *Ibid.*, 13:125-126
35. *Ibid.*, 9:10
36. *Journal History*, July 12, 1865
37. *Journal History*, April 15, 1844; see also *Times and Seasons*, Vol. IV (December 1, 1842), pp. 24-25.
38. *Millennial Star*, XXVI (1876), pp. 744, 746. President Brigham Young stated on one occasion that every government eventually meets its downfall when it continues to hold democratic elections, and to work without the voice of God (see JD 14:93). John Taylor stated that in a democratic society "the voice of the people is frequently the voice of the Devil." (JD 7:326)
39. *Millennial Star*, V (1844), p. 150
40. JD 6:342
41. *Ibid.*, 6:346-347; see also Ibid., 3:71-73
42. Orson Pratt, *The Seer*, II, 266-267
43. JD 14:93
44. DHC 7:381-382
45. JD 20:204
46. DHC 7:382. This is not to say that these men will live and act in the Society of Zion (with its socio-economic and spiritual aspects). These men will probably reside in a free society like that of our democratic America, but enjoying the protection and security of the Kingdom of God. They will be required to recognize the will of the Lord as the final word.
47. Details concerning the collapse and fall of the nations of the earth will be considered in Chapter 7.
48. See D & C 45:67-68
49. JD 9:342; see also Ibid., 17:156-157
50. *Ibid.*, 9:343; see also Ibid., 1:230; Ibid., 3:71-73
51. *Ibid.*, 6:345-346
52. *Millennial Star* 10:81-88
53. JD 11:275; see also Ibid., 2:310, 316 Ibid., 3:16; Ibid., 7:142; Ibid., 12:274
54. *Ibid.*, 9:137-138; compare D & C 82:14

CHAPTER 6

PRIESTHOOD CORRELATION IN ZION

Any Latter-day Saint with vision cannot help but marvel at the major organizational changes and developments in the Church over the past decade. It is obvious to many Saints that the Almighty is preparing again a people for the establishment of Zion. As the time of the Second Advent draws near, the Living Oracles continue to introduce divine programs which will bring the Saints to a point where all are truly pure in heart, and thus qualified to greet the Savior at His coming.

A NEED FOR CORRELATION

On March 24, 1960 the First Presidency of the Church sent a letter to the Melchizedek Priesthood Committee, of which Elder Harold B. Lee was the chairman. This letter asked that the Priesthood Committee consider the need of the Church to undertake the following:

1. A correlation of priesthood and auxiliary curricula. This proceeding was to avoid duplication, add efficiency, and ensure that the Saints are taught the doctrines in a way that would build testimonies and allegiance to the Church.
2. Preparation of courses of study with an eye toward the major functions of that particular priesthood quorum or auxiliary organization.

3. Coordination and correlation of all activities and programs of priesthood quorums and auxiliary organizations.

To accomplish these ends, the First Presidency and Council of the Twelve established an all-Church coordinating council and three coordinating committees: one for the children, one for the youth, and one for adults. This council and the three committees had the responsibility of correlating the total instructional and activity programs of all auxiliaries and quorums. The specific function of the all-Church coordinating council was to formulate policy which would govern the planning, writing, coordination, and implementation of the entire Church curriculum. [1] Elder Lee stated that the adoption of such a program would lead to "...the consolidation and simplification of church curricula, church publications, church buildings, church meetings, and many other important aspects of the Lord's work." [2]

CORRELATION AND THE FAMILY

At the General Priesthood Meeting in April of 1963 Elder Harold B. Lee introduced to the Church the concept of "Home Teaching," as a divine new program to supplement the old program of Ward Teaching; the responsibility of the priesthood to "watch over the Church" was given greater stress. The role of the program of Home Teaching in priesthood correlation is seen only when one views the true role of the home teacher as the connecting link between the family and the Ward organization; it is through the home teacher that home and church activities are correlated. Though much gospel training and development are made possible through the auxiliaries and quorums, still the greatest responsibility for developing gospel scholarship and conviction rests upon the parents.

The First Presidency made the following statement in 1963:

> *The home is the basis of a righteous life and no other instrumentality can take its place nor fulfil its essential functions;* the utmost the auxiliaries can do is to aid the home *in its problems, giving special aid and succor where such is necessary.* . . . [3]

CORRELATION IN THE WARD

On the Ward level, all activities and programs are coordinated through correlation committee meetings. The Priesthood Executive Correlation Committee consists of all priesthood leaders, and exists to coordinate all activities between quorums of the priesthood. This group is expanded to include the Presidencies of auxiliaries and thus becomes the Ward Council Correlation Committee. Through these two committees all programs in the Ward are correlated to insure communication and efficiency, and to avoid duplication of effort. Through Ward correlation the interests of all Ward members and Ward organizations are represented and considered.

THE ROLE OF AUXILIARIES

Each of the auxiliary organizations serves specific needs of the Saints. The Aaronic Priesthood MIA (Mutual Improvement Association) and Melchizedek Priesthood MIA (Mutual Interests Association) have been given to teach the doctrines of the Church, but also to meet the social and cultural needs of the individual. It is through the MIA that young people and adults learn valuable interpersonal skills. It is through the MIA that young people and adults learn recreational and cultural skills. And it is through the MIA that all Saints learn to appreciate a social order with a spiritual basis, and one that will prepare them for the social order of Zion.

The Primary and Sunday School organizations exist for teaching the gospel to youth and adults of the Ward, and thus supplementing the teaching of the home. It is through Primary and Sunday School that all may learn to stand up proudly and say, ''I am a child of God.''

The Relief Society of women exists to build skills in the areas of cultural refinement, homemaking, and spirituality. The sisters of the Church are taught lessons and given specific training in how to be more creative in meeting the family's needs. The most important training the woman receives in Relief Society is how she may become a true helpmeet to her husband, and how she may more effectively abide by his law in righteousness. Just as Priesthood training prepares a man to assume his rightful position as a King and Priest over his posterity, so also does the Relief Society organization seek to prepare righteous women to be Queens and Priestesses to their husbands.

All auxiliaries are correlated by and under the jurisdiction of the Priesthood. As the period of time is accelerated preparatory to the ushering in of the millennial kingdom, more and more responsibility for teaching and training will come under the auspices of the priesthood. In the spirit of prophecy, President Joseph F. Smith spoke concerning that day:

> We expect to see the day, if we live long enough (and if some of us do not live long enough to see it, there are others who will), when every council of the priesthood in the Church of Jesus Christ of Latter-day Saints will understand its duty; will assume its own responsibility, will magnify its calling, and fill its place in the Church, to the utmost, according to the intelligence and ability possessed by it. When that day shall come there will not be so much necessity for work that is now being done by the auxiliary organizations, because it will be done by the regular quorums of the priesthood.[4]

THE LAW OF THE GOSPEL

The Priesthood Welfare Program provides a means of caring for each other in the spiritual, temporal, and social realms of life. King Benjamin taught that the only way to retain a remission of sins from day to day is by caring for the spiritual and temporal needs of those about us.[5] The General Welfare Program of the Church contains three broad sub-systems which operate to care for the ''whole'' person. General Welfare is that part of the Welfare Plan which insures that the Saints are fed, clothed, and able to obtain an honorable wage. Health Services deals with the medical care and health facilities available to all members. Social Services deals with solving mental and emotional problems, building interpersonal skills, and rehabilitating those who desire to return to active participation in society.

When the time comes that the Saints truly become one in all things (social, economic, spiritual) through the powers of the Holy Ghost, then the Church will stand independent of the world. The Welfare Program will be one of the means of preparing the Latter-day Saints to live fully the Law of Consecration and Stewardship. President J. Reuben Clark explained that

> . . .in many of its great essentials, we have, as the Welfare Plan has now developed, the broad essentials of the United Order. *Furthermore, having in mind the assistance which is being given from time to time and in various wards to help set people up in business or in farming, we have a plan which is not essentially unlike that which was in the United Order when the poor were given portions from the common fund.* [6]

Although we shall be equal and united in all things, it is probable that the Welfare Plan will not be done away completely, but that some aspect of the program (Health and Social Services) will be retained because of their utility.

We thus see that through living the Law of the Gospel the Saints are made ready for the Lord's Law of Economics in the Society of Zion.

EXALTING THE FAMILY

The program of Priesthood Home Teaching is a vital one in establishing a Zion people in these last days. Very few home teachers understand fully their role to care for the spiritual and temporal needs of the family; few realize fully their role as the connecting link between the Melchizedek Order and the Patriarchal Order. The home teacher is responsible to have the knowledge and power necessary to "teach them the word of God with all diligence."[7] His major role, however, lies in ensuring that the family father is maturing spiritually to the point where he can serve as a true Patriarch to the home. In this sense, then, the home teacher is a "Patriarch builder."

The Family Home Evening Program is another means of strengthening the family. The family is the basis of the Divine Patriarchal Order, and is the only unit which will exist in Celestial society. It is in the home that spiritual guidance must be given if family solidarity is to be maintained. President Joseph F. Smith said:

> Do not let your children out to specialists in these things, but teach them by your own precept and example, by your own fireside. Be a specialist yourself in the truth. *Let our meetings, schools and organizations, instead of being our only or leading teachers, be supplements to our teaching and training in the home. Not one child in a hundred would go astray, if the home environment, example and training, were in harmony with the truth in the gospel of Christ, as revealed and taught to the Latter-day Saints.*[8]

In addition to uniting families, the Family Home Evening helps to establish the father as patriarch over his posterity; it thus aids the father in becoming the source of light and truth to his family. Fathers and mothers may thus establish a millennial kingdom within the walls of their own home.

Priesthood Genealogy is an important aspect of the Family Exaltation Program, in which we labor to exalt the dead as well as the living. Joseph Smith taught that "The greatest responsibility in this world that God has laid upon us is to seek after our dead."[9] The Apostle Paul taught the Ephesian Saints that ". . .in the dispensation of the fulness of times he (Christ) might gather together in one all things in Christ, both which are in heaven, and which are on earth; even in him."[10] To gather all things (in heaven and on earth) together in Christ is to perfect the Patriarchal Order on earth *and in heaven.* To perfect this Holy Order in heaven is to provide the means whereby our kindred dead may be washed, annointed, endowed, and sealed in the Temple of God. Elder ElRay L. Christiansen urged every man and woman to seek out their dead and complete the family line.

> *Every man should consider this his first duty. . . .*
> *families, united eternally, are the primary purpose of all*
> *life. It is the duty of every man to see to it that the records*
> *of his progenitors are obtained, and. . . that the or-*
> *dinances necessary for salvation and exaltation are ad-*
> *ministered in behalf of his kindred dead.*[11]

Through the program of Priesthood Genealogy we are able to exalt *families* and thus aid in the establishment of the perfected kingdom.

A WARNING TO THE NATIONS

The Savior's declaration to the original Twelve to "Go ye therefore and teach all nations. . ."[12] has been echoed in these latter days:

*And ye shall go forth in the power of my Spirit,
preaching my gospel, two by two, in my name, lifting up
your voices as with the sound of a trump, declaring my
word like unto angels of God.*[13]

The powerful missionary program of the Church exists in
order to build up Zion by gathering Israel. One of the
promises to Father Abraham was that his seed would bear
the ministry to all nations of the earth,[14] and it is through
the House of Israel that the pure in heart are gathered into
the Society of Zion. Another important purpose of the
Priesthood Missionary Program is to warn the nations of the
impending judgements that await the unrepentant.

*And the voice of warning shall be unto all people, by
the mouths of my disciples, whom I have chosen in these
last days.*
*And they shall go forth and none shall stay them, for
I the Lord have commanded them.*[15]

Again, the Lord said that it ". . .becometh every man who
hath been warned to warn his neighbor."[16] Finally, the
missionary program will be one of the means by which the
nations of the earth will turn their attention to Zion as an
ensign of righteousness and stability. As the social systems
and governments of the world crumble and fall, the
Kingdom of God will stand. This power of example will
serve as a tremendous missionary tool.

SUMMARY

Through the program of Priesthood Correlation all
curricula and activities of the quorums and auxiliaries are
coordinated. Through the auxiliaries of the Church, the
members learn the doctrines of the Kingdom, as well as
valuable skills. The Priesthood Home Teaching, Family
Home Evening, and Family Exaltation Programs provide

the means for establishing the Divine Patriarchal Order. Through Priesthood Welfare the temporal, social, and spiritual needs of all members are met, and the Saints are prepared (by living the Law of the Gospel) eventually to enter into the Law of Consecration and Stewardship. Through the Priesthood Missionary Program Israel is gathered, the nations of the earth are warned of impending judgements, and Zion is proclaimed as the Divine Standard. Thus by means of an overall plan of correlation, under the arm of the priesthood, the Lord is preparing again a people who will be united in heavenly and earthly things.

CHAPTER 6
—FOOTNOTES—

1. Harold B. Lee, 131st Semi-annual CR, General Priesthood Meeting, Sept. 30, 1961, pp. 77-82. See also IE 65:34-37 (January, 1961).
2. *Ibid.*
3. Harold B. Lee, 133rd Annual CR, General Priesthood Meeting, April 6, 1963, pp. 79-89. See also IE 66:500-505 (June, 1963).
4. CR, April 1906. See also Joseph F. Smith, *Gospel Doctrine*, Deseret Book Company, 1971, p. 159.
5. Mosiah 4
6. CR, October 1942, pp. 57-58.
7. Jacob 1:19
8. Joseph F. Smith, *Gospel Doctrine*, p. 302.
9. TPJS, p. 356
10. Ephesians 1:10
11. ElRay L. Christiansen, "A Foundation Stone of the Gospel," IE 65:957 (December, 1962).
12. Matthew 28:19; Mark 16:15
13. D & C 42:6
14. Abraham 2:9
15. D & C 1:4-5. A more detailed consideration of the impending judgements will be undertaken in Chapter 7.
16. *Ibid.*, 88:81

CHAPTER 7

THE KINGDOM OF GOD AND THE FUTURE

To this point we have considered some of the qualities of Zions in times past, some of the spiritual preparations necessary in establishing Zion among the Saints once again, and also some of the modern organizational developments of the present day that are preparing the people for the full program of the kingdom of God. This chapter will be devoted to the prophetic picture of the Kingdom, and will deal specifically with a few of the many events incident to the Lord's Coming in glory.

SPIRIT OF GOD TO BE WITHDRAWN

The world is fast approaching the state of abomination that was prevalent in the wicked cities of Sodom and Gomorrah. As the people of the earth continue to deny the Master, the wrath of a just God will begin to be made known. The Lord Himself explained that if man does not repent, ". . .from him shall be taken even the light which he has received; for my spirit shall not always strive with man, saith the Lord of Hosts." [1] A natural consequence of sin is the withdrawal of the Spirit of God. [2] Just as the Spirit of the Lord has certain evident influences on man, so does its absence or withdrawal have visible effects: it appears that the withdrawal of the Spirit has exactly opposite effects on a body of people than the endowment of this sacred influence. Void of the Spirit, man has no desire to deal justly with his fellow beings, but instead is full of desire for lying, cheating, and degrading. Also, instead of entering into righteous and loyal unions, the aspiritual man seeks to aggrandize self at the expense of others. Perhaps the only types of union characteristic of this calibre of beings are the secret combinations, which seek to destroy the works of God. In the words of Paul, these types of men are "Without natural affections, trucebreakers, false accusers, incontinent, fierce, despisers of those that are good."[3]

Left to himself, man cannot maintain a profitable existence. Without the Spirit of the Lord man cannot love deeply, for this quality of love has its source in Christ, [4] and without the love of Christ, it is thus impossible to maintain a peaceful existence—war and destruction are natural consequences. The Prophet Joseph Smith spoke firmly in October of 1843:

> *I prophesy, in the name of the Lord God of Israel, anguish and wrath and tribulation and the* withdrawing of the Spirit of God from the earth *await this generation, until they are visited with utter desolation.* [5]

President Wilford Woodruff also recognized the Lord's intentions in removing His influence from man when he said, "The Lord is withdrawing His Spirit from the nations of the earth, and the power of the devil is gaining dominion over the children of men." [6] President John Taylor likewise discussed the reason for the dreadful fate of many nations:

> *Why is it that thrones will be cast down, empires dissolved, nations destroyed, and confusions and distress cover all people, as the prophets have spoken?* Because the Spirit of the Lord will be withdrawn from the nations *in consequence of their wickedness, and they will be left to their own folly.* [7]

WAR TO BE POURED OUT.

As early as 1832 the Prophet Joseph Smith gave to the world a great prophecy on war. Some of this prophecy is recorded as follows:

> *Verily, thus saith the Lord concerning the* wars *that will shortly come to pass, beginning at the rebellion of South Carolina, which will eventually terminate in the death and misery of many souls;*
>
> And the time will come that war will be poured out upon all nations, *beginning at this place.*
>
> *For behold, the Southern States shall be divided against the Northern States, and the Southern States will call on other nations, even the nation of Great Britain, as it is called, and* they shall also call upon other nations, *in order to defend themselves against other nations; and* then *shall war be poured out upon all nations.* [8]

At least six salient points with regard to this excerpt of scripture are worth noting.

1. The revelation cited made reference to the beginning of an era of warfare and *wars* to follow. It was not limited in scope to the Civil War in the 1860's. [9]

2. This era of warfare would begin at the rebellion of South Carolina.

3. The rebellion of South Carolina would serve as the "beginning of the end," for the Lord stated later in the same revelation (verse 6) that such a state of warfare and destruction would continue until an end to all nations had been made.

4. The Southern States would wage war against the Northern States and vice versa.

5. The Southern Sates would request the assistance of other nations, specifically, Great Britain.

6. Great Britain would call upon other nations for

assistance in order to defend herself against her enemies. After this, war would be poured out upon all nations.

Since the Civil War the world has been vexed constantly by bloodshed and warfare, for there has been no peace on earth. Such a state will continue until the end of the world or destruction of the wicked, for the Lord has told us that one of the signs of His Coming will be a day filled with wars and rumors of wars.[10] At that point in which Great Britain requested assistance in her war efforts (World War I) world-wide war was initiated. And thus war will be poured out upon all nations until the end of time, at which time the Prince of Peace will reign.[11]

KINGDOMS OF THE EARTH TO COLLAPSE.

As war and destruction are spread throughout the world, the kingdoms of man will begin to lose power over their subjects. Not only will there be wars between nations, but also wars between states, cities, and communities; again, this is in consequence of the withdrawal of the Lord's Spirit. Elder Orson Pratt spoke of this conditon of internal warfare:

> it will be very different from the war between the North and the South .... It will be a war of neighborhood against neighborhood, city against city, town against town, county against county, state against state, and they will go forth, destroying and being destroyed. ...[12]

The fateful message of the prophets is that the United States of America will not escape these conditions. The wickedness in America is fast approaching its fulness, and thus the same judgements are due this nation. Joseph Smith therefore wrote in 1833:

> *And now I am prepared to say by the authority of Jesus Christ, that not many years shall pass away before* the United States shall present such a scene of bloodshed as has not a parallel in the history of our nation. . . . [13]

Joseph described a condition in which he ". . .saw men hunting the lives of their own sons, and brother murdering brother, women killing their own daughters, and daughters seeking the lives of their mothers." [14] President Taylor said:

> This nation and other nations will be overthrown, *not because of their virtue, but because of their corruption and iniquity. The time will come, for the prophecies will be fulfilled, when kingdoms will be destroyed, thrones cast down, and the powers of the earth shaken, and God's wrath will be kindled against the nations of the earth* [15]

Speaking specifically concerning this country, President Wilford Woodruff spoke soberly:

> *When I contemplate the conditon of our nation and see that wickedness and abominations are increasing, so much so that the whole heavens groan and weep over the abominations of this nation and the nations of the earth, I ask myself the question,* can the American nation escape? The answer comes, No; its destruction, as well as the destruction of the world, is sure; *just as sure as the Lord cut off and destroyed the two great and prosperous nations that once inhabited this continent of North and South America, because of their wickedness, so will He them destroy, and sooner or later they will reap the fruits of their own wicked acts and be numbered among the past.* [16]

The destruction of the American Nation will extend to all aspects of life, including the political programs of man. As the Spirit of Satan reigns rampant in the land, the social systems as well as local and national government will fall. Joseph Smith was reported to have said that "mobs will not decrease, but will increase until the whole government becomes a mob. . . ."[17] He further stated on another occasion that this nation would come to an end, ". . .if she continues to disregard the cries of her virtuous citizens, as she has done and is now doing."[18] Elder Orson Pratt declared:

> *God has sent forth his warning message in the midst of this nation, but they have rejected it and treated his servants with contempt; the Lord has gathered out his people from their midst, and has planted them here in these mountains; and he will speedily fulfill the prophecy in relation to the overthrow of this nation, and their destruction. . . mobocracy will prevail and their (sic) will be no security, through this great Republic, for the lives or property of the people.[19]*

Thus, in fulfillment of Daniel's prophecy, the day will come when the kingdoms of men will "break in pieces" and be no more.[20]

A GATHERING IN THE MOUNTAINS.

As this scene of disruption spreads across the globe and the nations of the earth lose their powers, it will become apparent to the Saints everywhere that they must "flee to Zion."[21] This aspect of the prophetic picture is beautifully stated in a hymn by Richard Smith:

> *Israel, Israel, God is calling,*
> *Calling thee from lands of woe:*
> *Babylon the great is falling.*
> *God shall all her towers o'er-throw.*
> Come to Zion, come to Zion
> Ere his floods of anger flow.

Come to Zion, come to Zion
Ere his floods of anger flow

Israel! Israel! Canst thou linger
Still in error's gloomy ways?
Mark how judgement's pointing finger
Justifies no vain delays.
Come to Zion, come to Zion!
Zion's walls shall ring with praise.
Come to Zion, Come to Zion!
Zion's walls shall ring with praise. [22]

From the above, we see that the cry to gather to Zion will go forth to the House of Israel. Brigham Young described the Salt Lake valley as a place of security and refuge. He spoke of the valley as ". . .the place in which the Lord designed to hide his people. . . . It has been designed, for many generations, to hide up the Saints in the last days, until the indignation of the Almighty be over."[23] Elder Orson Pratt also joyed in the fact that ". . .there is still a place left in the heart of the American continent where there are peace and safety and refuge from the storms, desolations and tribulations coming upon the wicked."[24] With the scattered Saints will come the righteous Gentiles who desire security and protection from the storms of chaos. This gathering of the Gentiles to the Rockies was prophesied by Orson Pratt:

A flowing stream is one that runs continually; and the Gentiles will, at that day, come to us as a flowing stream. . . . *The people will see that the hand of God is over this people; they will see that He is in our midst, and that He is our watchtower, that He is our shield and our defense, and therefore, they will say, "Let us go up and put our riches in Zion, for there is no safety in our own nations."* [25]

One of the great functions of Zion in the mountains will be to uphold the divinely inspired principles of constitutional government. Joseph Smith was reported to have prophesied concerning the time when the constitution of the United States ''would hang, as it were, by a single thread.'' [26] Elder Orson Hyde reported concerning the Prophet's statements

I believe he said something like this—that the time would come when the Constitution and the country would be in danger of an overthrow; and said he, if the Constitution be saved at all, *it will be by the Elders of this Church.* [27]

We are to understand that when the Government of God is established in Zion, the Elders of the Church will proclaim the truths of the Constitution that existed before it became amended and prostituted by the Gentiles. We are nowhere given to understand that the Priesthood of God will migrate to the nation's capital to rebuild the government, but only that the Elders will stand firmly for the Constitution in the Kingdom of God.

When the people shall have torn to shreds the Constitution of the United States, the elders of Israel will be found holding it up to the nations of the earth *and proclaiming liberty and equal rights to all men and extending the hand of fellowship to the oppressed of all nations.* [28]

THE MOVE TO JACKSON COUNTY

As the era of universal chaos continues among the peoples of the world, the Saints, at one point, will begin the return to Independence. Orson Pratt said that ''when the time shall come that the Lord shall waste away this nation, he will give commandment to this people to return and possess their own inheritance which they purchased some forty-four years ago in the state of Missouri." [29] Though the trek east will be extremely hazardous and difficult, [30] the power of the Lord will rest mightily upon the Saints. Elder Orson Pratt described the trek in the following way:

> We shall go back to Jackson County. . . . when we go back, there will be a very large organization consisting of thousands, and tens of thousands, and they will march forward, the glory of the Lord overshadowing their camp by day in the form of a cloud, and a pillar of flaming fire by night, the Lord's voice being uttered forth before his army. . . . [31]

As the people of God make their way to the land of their inheritance, the way will be made clear, for the Almighty will "raise up unto my people a man, who shall lead them like as Moses led the children of Israel." [32]

It is not expected that all of the Saints will make the eastward journey to Missouri, for many will be asked to remain in the West to maintain Zion there. President Brigham Young spoke of this situation.

> Are we going back to Jackson County? Yes. When? As soon as the way opens up. Are we all going? O no! Of course not. The country is not large enough to hold our present numbers. When we do return there, will there be any less remaining in these mountains than we number today? No, there may be a hundred then for every single one that is there now. [33]

Similarly, Elder Pratt stated that "We do not expect that when the time shall come, that all Latter-day Saints, who now occupy the mountain valleys, will go in one consolidated body. . . . We do not expect any such thing." [34]

THE NEW JERUSALEM

Once the Saints arrive in the Missouri area, they shall begin to rebuild the area,[35] and thus establish a new Zion. The building of Zion will be undertaken, according to the Prophet Joseph, ". . .by the counsel of Jehovah, by the revelations of heaven. . . ."[36] Similarly, President John Taylor said "We will build up our Zion after the pattern that God will show us, and we will be governed by His law and submit to His authority and be governed by the Holy Priesthood and by the word and will of God."[37] The Lord made clear to the Nephites *who* would be involved in the building of the complex of cities called the New Jerusalem when He said: "And they (the Gentiles) shall assist my people, the remnant of Jacob, and also as many of the house of Israel as shall come, that they may build a city, which shall be called the New Jerusalem."[38] Christ here lists three groups of people who will join in the building of the city:

1. As many of the House of Israel as will come. This, of course, includes the members of the Church, and probably the Ten Tribes, who will have returned.[39]

2. The remnants of Jacob. After the Lamanites have been converted in mass to the Church,[40] they will assist in the building program. Orson Pratt explained that "they (the Lamanites) will also be instructed to cultivate the earth, to build temples as we do, . . . and then after having received this information and instruction, we shall have the privilege of helping them to build the New Jerusalem."[41] "The remnants of Jacob" also refers to all of the House of Israel (as considered in point one above). President Joseph Fielding Smith therefore stated that "The remnant of the house of Israel spoken of . . . does not only have reference to the descendants of Lehi, but all of the house of Israel, the children of Jacob. . . ."[42]

3. The Gentiles or Christian nations. [43] Thus the Lord explained that He would soften the hearts of the kings and rulers, ". . .that they may come to the light of truth, and the Gentiles to the exaltation of lifting up of Zion." [44]

The people of Zion will be those who desire to sanctify themselves through living the laws of the Celestial Kingdom. The Saints in Missouri will be under covenant to consecrate their all to the Lord through the Divine Law of Economics; this is a necessary step before Zion can exist completely on earth. [45] Orson Pratt explained that the Law of Consecration and Stewardship would be among the first teachings given in Zion. [46] President Wilford Woodruff declared in 1874:

> *Jesus will never receive the Zion of God unless its people are united according to celestial law, for all who go into the presence of God have to go there by this law. Enoch had to practice this law, and we shall have to do the same if we are ever accepted of God as he was. It has been promised that* the New Jerusalem will be built up in our day and generation, and it will have to be done by the United Order of Zion and according to celestial law. [47]

The powers of the Spirit will be so evident that the glory of the Lord will be seen for miles around. Orson Pratt thus prophesied that "The light will shine so conspicuously from that city, extending to the very heavens, that it will in reality be like unto a city set upon a hill that cannot be hid. . . ." [48] Not only will the Saints of God be imbued with the Holy Spirit, but the elements of the earth, including the buildings in the area, will be immortalized, so as to stand forever. [49] President John Taylor spoke of the glorious state of Zion:

> *...when the time comes that these calamities we read of*
> *shall overtake the earth,* those that are prepared will have
> the power of translation, *as they had in former times, and*
> *the city will be translated.*[50]

President Taylor said on another occasion that ". . .the
people, from the President down, will all be under the
guidance and direction of the Lord in all the pursuits of
human life; until eventually they will be enabled to erect
cities that will be fit to be caught up. . . ."[51]

THE TEN TRIBES RETURN

In 975 B.C., the division between Judah and Israel
occurred, the ten tribes (Israel) refusing to follow the
Davidic line of kings any longer. Instead of following
Rehoboam, the son of Solomon, these tribes appointed an
Ephraimite, Jeroboam, as their king. The two groups
maintained a separate existence for over two hundred years.
In 721 B.C., the tribes of Israel were taken captive by the
Assyrians, under the direction of Shalmaneser. Some time
after this event these tribes escaped to the North and were
never again heard from. To this day they have maintained an
isolated existence, so that only the Lord has a knowledge as
to their exact location.

A careful search of statements by some early brethren
in the Church helps us to understand somewhat the state of
the Lost Tribes. We understand from Orson Pratt, for
example, that God raised up Prophets among this
group.[52] Joseph   Smith   was   reported   to   have
". . .prophesied that John the Revelator was then among
the Ten Tribes of Israel who had been led away by
Shalmaneser, king of Assyria, to prepare them for their
return from their long dispersion, to again possess the land
of their fathers."[53] Orson Pratt likewise explained that
". . . John the Revelator will be there, teaching, instructing

and preparing them for this great work."[54] Elder Pratt
explained on another occasion that the Ten Tribes would
have Twelve Apostles among them to meet the Lord when
He comes to the New Jerusalem.[55]   That the Lost Tribes
have some degree of priesthood is evident from the following
by Brother Pratt:

> God is determined to raise up Prophets among that
> people, but he will not bestow upon them all the fulness of
> the blessings of the Priesthood. The fulness will be
> reserved to be given to them after they come to Zion. But
> Prophets will be among them while in the north, and a
> portion of the Priesthood will be there. . . .[56]

This statement seems to clarify the fact that the Ten Tribes
will come to Zion in order to receive a fulness of priesthood,
which fulness they do not now enjoy. Thus the Master
explained in a revelation given in 1831 that the Lost Tribes
would ". . . fall down and be crowned with glory, even in
Zion, by the hands of the servants of the Lord, even the
children of Ephraim."[57]   It is at this time that Israel will be
given the higher sealing blessings of the temple. President
Wilford Woodruff therefore spoke of the Ten Tribes
receiving priesthood powers and their endowments on this
occasion.[58]

The location of this branch of Israel remains a mystery,
except for numerous references to the fact that the Tribes
are in the North. There are those, however, who have
attempted to give us some knowledge of their state and
whereabouts. Brigham Young taught that "the Ten Tribes
of Israel are on a portion of the earth—a portion separate
from the main land."[59] More specifically, Elder Parley P.
Pratt spoke concerning some events just incident to the
Lord's coming:

> The stars which will fall to the earth are meteors,
> fragments which have been broken off from the earth

from time to time, *in the mighty convulsions of nature. Some in the days of Enoch, some perhaps in the days of Peleg,* some with the ten tribes, *and some at the crucifixion of the Messiah.* These all must be restored again *at the "times of restitution of ALL THINGS."* This will restore the ten tribes of Israel, *and also bring again Zion, even Enoch's city. . . . When these fragments (some of which are vastly larger than the present earth) are brought back and joined to this earth, it will cause a convulsion of all nature. . . . The earth will be much larger than it is now.*[60]

A similar statement was made by Daniel Allen, a member of the Parowan School of the Prophets. Allen reported a conversation which he had with the Prophet Joseph Smith:

I heard Joseph the Prophet say that he had seen John the Revelator and had a long conversation with him, who told him that he John was their leader, Prophet, Priest and King And Said that he was preparing that people to return, And Further said there is a mighty host of us, And Joseph Further said that men might hunt for them but they could not find them for they were upon a portion of this planet that had been broken off *and which was taken away and the sea rushed in between Europe and America, and that when that piece returned there would be a great shake the sea would then move to the north where it belonged in the morning of creation. (sic)*[61]

CHRIST TO VISIT THE NEW JERUSALEM

As the glory of the Lord continues to grow in intensity, the Modern Zion will become the light of the world. The Lord Himself explained that ". . .the powers of heaven shall be in the midst of this people; yea, even I will be in the midst of you."[62]   Though without doubt the Lord will have appeared to many of the pure in heart already,[63]   we are to understand that the first official visit of the Christ to an organized body of Saints will be His sudden appearance in His Temple. In a revelation given to Edward Partridge in December of 1830 the Lord said: "I am Jesus Christ, the Son of God; wherefore, gird up your loins and *I will suddenly come to my temple.*[64]   The Savior explained on a later occasion that inasmuch as the Saints build a house unto Him and maintain their purity, that His glory would rest upon it.[65]   He further stated that ". . .my presence shall be there, for I will come into it, And all the pure in heart that shall come into it shall see God.''[66]   Elder Orson Pratt described this great event as follows:

> *It shall come to pass that* every man and every woman who is pure in heart, who shall go inside of that temple, will see the Lord. *Now, how great a blessing it will be to see the Lord of Hosts as we see one another in the flesh.*[67]

We are not told exactly who is to be in attendance at the time of this momentous appearance; we only know that many of the pure in heart will be privileged to see the Master on that occasion.

The next major appearance of the Savior in the New Jerusalem seems to be His appearance at the Priesthood Council at Adam-Ondi-Ahman, or Spring Hill, Missouri.[68]   Daniel prophesied that he ". . .beheld till the thrones were cast down (i.e., the kingdoms of the world fell to the dust), and the Ancient of days (Adam) did sit, . . . and ten thousand times ten thousand stood before him: the judgement was set, and the books were opened.''[69]   Joseph Smith spoke of Daniel's account as follows:

> *. . .Father Adam, Michael, . . .will call his children together and hold a council with them to prepare them for the coming of the Son of Man. He (Adam) is the father of the human family, and presides over the spirits of all men, and* all that have had the keys must stand before him

> *in this grand council. . . . The son of Man stands before*
> *him and there is given him (Christ) glory and dominion.*
> *Adam delivers up his stewardship to Christ. . . .''*[70]

Elder Orson Pratt commented further as to the proceedings
of the great Council. Speaking of Father Adam, Pratt said:

> *He comes* to set in order the councils of the Priesthood
> pertaining to all dispensations, *to arrange the Priesthood*
> *and the councils of the Saints of all former dispensations*
> *in one grand family and household. . . . Then every*
> *family that is in the order of the Priesthood, and* every
> man and every woman, and every son or daughter
> whatever their kindred, descent or Priesthood, will know
> their place.[71]

This Priesthood Council, which will remain a secret to the
Church at large,[72] seems, therefore, to serve three main
functions:

    1. All who have held keys of priesthood authority will
turn these keys over to Father Adam.

    2. The Councils of the priesthood through all
dispensations are set in order, so that all men, women, and
children may know their place.

    3. Christ is crowned as King and given all glory and
dominion.

CHRIST'S COMING IN GLORY

    Although Christ will have appeared many times to the
Saints in Missouri, yet the people of the world will be totally
unaware of such events. His coming in glory and power to
all the earth will be as "a thief in the night," for no man
knows the exact hour of this coming.[73] There are,
however, certain events just incident to this final appearance
that will alert the pure in heart as to the nearness of His

coming. The Master taught the original Twelve that one of these events was the "sign of the Son of Man."[74] Though the writers of the New Testament are unclear as to what this sign will be, the Prophet Joseph commented as follows:

> . . . *then will appear one grand* sign of the Son of Man *in heaven. But what will the world do? They will say it is a planet, a comet, etc, But the Son of Man will come as the sign of the coming of the Son of Man, which will be as the light of the morning cometh out of the east.* [75]

It appears from the Prophet's description that this "sign" will resemble that of a planet or comet approaching the earth. It is highly probably that such is the case, for Wandle Mace explained that the Prophet Joseph taught that this sign is simply the return of the city of Enoch to the earth.[76] As the people of the world shake with fear and uncertainty, the people of God will rejoice at the descent of the ancient Zion. As Enoch's Zion descends, the Latter-day Zion will ascend, and the peoples of each will meet with joy and thanksgiving. President John Taylor spoke of this moving event:

> . . . *those that are prepared will have the power of translation, as they had in former times, and the city (New Jerusalem) will he translated. And* Zion that is on the earth will rise, and the Zion above will descend, *as we are told, and* we will meet and fall on each other's necks and embrace and kiss each other. *And thus the purposes of God to a certain extent will then be fulfilled.* [77]

On another occasion, President Taylor spoke in a similar vein:

> . . . *we are told in latter revelation in relation to these matters that a Zion will be built up in our day: . . . and that when the time arrives, the Zion that was caught up*

will descend, and the Zion that will be organized here will ascend, both possessed of the same spirit, *their peoples having been preserved by the power of God according to His purposes and as His children, to take part in the events of the latter days. We are told that when the people of these two Zions meet, they will fall on each others' necks, and embrace and kiss each other.*[78]

The Lord explained in a revelation given in September of 1832 that those filled with a knowledge of God will then "see eye to eye," and will all sing a *new song:*

> *The Lord hath brought again Zion;*
> *The Lord hath redeemed his people, Israel,*
> *According to the election of his grace,*
> *Which was brought to pass by the faith*
> *And covenant of their fathers.*
>
> *The Lord hath redeemed his people;*
> *And Satan is bound and time is no longer.*
> *The Lord hath gathered all things in one.*
> The Lord hath brought down Zion from above.
> The Lord hath brought up Zion from beneath.
>
> *The earth hath travailed and brought forth her strength;*
> *And truth is established in her bowels;*
> *And the heavens have smiled upon her;*
> *And she is clothed with the glory of her God:*
> *For he stands in the midst of his people.*
>
> *Glory, and honor, and power, and might,*
> *Be ascribed to our God; for he is full of mercy,*
> *Justice, grace and truth, and peace.*
> *Forever and ever, Amen.*[79]

Those Saints on the earth who are pure in heart will be caught up to meet Christ at His coming. These only (the Saints) will be quickened[80] by the powers of the Holy

Spirit, so as to be capable of abiding the glory of the Savior. Zion will thus receive its King, and He shall reign whose right it is to reign.

SUMMARY

As the nations of the earth continue in their abominable practices, the Spirit of the Lord will gradually be withdrawn. As this withdrawal becomes more and more pronounced, its effects become evident in such things as strife, wars, and the eventual downfall of the kingdoms of the world. As the era of chaos continues, the Saints and righteous Gentiles will gather to the mountains for protection and security. Eventually many of the Saints will make the Eastward trek to Jackson County, Missouri, where they will build up the New Jerusalem. This complex of cities will be filled with the Spirit of the Lord to such an extent that the entire area will be worthy to be translated and caught up to meet the Zion of Enoch, just preceding the coming of the Master in glory. When Christ comes in His power and glory, the worthy Saints will be quickened and made ready to dwell in His presence for the period of the Millennium. Christ will then rule and reign as King of Kings and Lord of Lords.

CHAPTER 7
—FOOTNOTES—

1. D & C 1:33; compare Genesis 6:3; 2 Nephi 26:11; Moses 8:17
2. D & C 19:20; Alma 34:35
3. 2 Timothy 3:3
4. Moroni 7:47-48
5. DHC 6:58
6. JD 22:175
7. *Ibid.*, 6:24
8. D & C 87:1-3
9. See a statement by Elder Charles A. Callis in CR, April 1923, p. 22.
10. Matthew 24:6; Joseph Smith 1:28
11. JD 6:25; DHC 5:212
12. JD 20:151
13. DHC 1:315
14. DHC 3:390-391. See also JD 2:146-147; JD 20:150-151
15. JD 17:4
16. *Ibid.*, 21:301
17. As reported by Brigham Young in DN, Vol. 11, No. 9, May 1, 1861.
18. DHC 4:89
19. DEN, Vol. 8, Number 265, October 8, 1875.
20. Daniel 2:44
21. D & C 45:68-69; Ibid., 133:12
22. "Israel, Israel, God is Calling." from Hymns of the Church of Jesus Christ of Latter-day Saints, 1962, p. 81
23. DN. Vol. 11, Number 9 May 1, 1861
24. JD 12:345
25. *Ibid.*, 3:16
26. *Ibid.*, 7:15; Ibid., 6:152; Ibid., 12:204; Ibid., 2:182
27. *Ibid.*, 6:152
28. John Taylor, Ibid., 21:8
29. DEN, Vol. 8, Number 265, October 2, 1875.
30. See Joseph F. Smith, JD 24:156-157
31. *Ibid.*, 15:364
32. D & C 103:16; See also JD 21:153; JD 15:362-363
33. JD 18:355-356
34. *Ibid.*, 21:149
35. That Jackson County will be swept clean with the rest of the nation is clear from Brigham Young in JD 9:270. See also *Prophetic Sayings of Heber C. Kimball to Amanda H. Wilcox*, Brigham Young University Library.
36. DHC 5:65
37. JD 21:253; Compare Ibid., 10:147
38. 3 Nephi 21:23
39. JD 14:349-350
40. 3 Nephi 21:26; See also JD 17:301-302; "Proclamation of the Twelve Apostles of the Church of Jesus Christ of Latter-day Saints," *Millennial Star*, October 22, 1845.
41. JD 17:301

42. *Doctrines of Salvation,* Vol. II, p. 248.
43. For evidence that the term "Gentile" is used to refer to the Christian nations (as contrasted with the heathen nations) see JD 7:186 and JD 18:339-340.
44. D & C 124:3,9
45. *Ibid.,* 105:1-5
46. JD 21:149-150
47. *Ibid.,* 17:250
48. *Ibid.,* 24:29
49. See Orson Pratt in Ibid., 24:25-26
50. *Ibid.,* 21:253
51. *Ibid.,* 10:147
52. *Ibid.,* 18:25; See also D & C 133:26
53. DHC 1:176; Compare D & C 77:14
54. JD 18:25
55. *Ibid.,* 17:187-188
56. *Ibid.,* 18:25
57. D & C 133:32
58. JD 4:231-232; see also Ibid., 18:38
59. As reported in Matthias Cowley's *Wilford Woodruff,* Book-craft, p. 448. Note also a poem by Eliza R. Snow on the same page of this work:
    And when the Lord saw fit to hide
    The ten lost tribes away,
    Thou, earth, was severed to provide
    The orb on which they stay.
60. *Millennial Star* 1:258
61. "Minutes of the School of the Prophets Held in Parowan 1868-1872." Manuscript in Brigham Young University Library. Typewritten copy, 1956, p. 169.
62. 3 Nephi 20:22; see also 21:25
63. See a statement by Lorenzo Snow from an address of June 12, 1901 in DN, June 15, 1901. Also cited in N. B. Lundwall (compiler), *Temples of the Most High,* Bookcraft, 1969.
64. D & C 36:8
65. *Ibid.,* 97:15
66. *Ibid.,* 97:16
67. JD 21:330
68. D & C 116; TPJS, p. 122
69. Daniel 7:9-10
70. TPJS, p. 157
71. JD 17:185-188
72. Joseph Fielding Smith, *The Way to Perfection,* The Genealogical Society, 1943, p. 291.
73. Matthew 24:36
74. *Ibid.,* 24:30; See D & C 88:93
75. TPJS, p. 287
76. Sayings of Joseph Smith as reported by those who claimed to hear him make the statements, "Joseph Smith Papers," Church Historian's Library, Salt Lake City, Utah.
77. JD 21:253; See also Ibid., 26:37; Ibid., 10:147
78. *Ibid.,* 25:305; See also Ibid., 17:180
79. D & C 84:99-102
80. *Ibid.,* 88:96; See also Orson Pratt in JD 16:319

CHAPTER 8

THE PERFECTED ORDER: A KINGDOM OF PRIESTS

The Apostle Paul taught that the purpose of the Church was for "...the perfecting of the Saints, for the work of the ministry, for the edifying of the body of Christ: till we all come in the unity of the faith. . . ." (Ephesians 4:11-12) It appears that after the Saints will have come to a unity of the faith, the role of the Church structure, with its various auxiliaries and organizational aids, will be minimal.[1]   In actuality, the Church is provided for man as a help in establishing the Patriarchal Order; eventually all keys for instructing and preparing the family in every aspect of life will center in the righteous father.

THE MELCHIZEDEK AND PATRIARCHAL ORDERS

The Church, with its emphasis on quorums and offices in the Priesthood is governed today through the keys of the Melchizedek Order. In a sense, the Melchizedek Order may be viewed figuratively as a great construction crew, earnestly at work in the construction of a glorious temple. The Divine Patriarchal Order might thus be compared to the temple under construction. In the Patriarchal Order the basic unit is the family. Perhaps the only office that exists within this latter program (if we might use the word "office") is that of *heir.* Each righteous man, with his family, is a legal heir to all that his father or Patriarch possesses, in addition to all that God possesses. In the perfected Patriarchal Order each man stands as a King and a Priest with his wife by his side as a Queen and a Priestess.[2]   President Brigham Young spoke of this state:

> *We understand that we are to be made kings and priests unto God; now if I be made the king and lawgiver to my family, and if I have many sons, and their sons will have sons, and so on, from generation to generation, and, in this way, I may become the father of many fathers, or the king of many kings. This will constitute every man a prince, king, lord, or whatever the Father sees fit to confer upon us.*[3]

The Holy (Melchizedek) Priesthood holds the right of presidency, and thus presides over the Patriarchal Order.[4]   Joseph Smith taught that all Priesthood is Melchizedek, but that there are different portions or degrees of it.[5]   Rights and privileges within the Patriarchal Order must therefore be sanctioned by the presiding High Priest in the Melchizedek Order.

THE PATRIARCHAL ORDER THROUGH THE AGES

Adam, the Ancient of Days, stands at the head of the human family, and as such is the great Patriarchal Head, under Christ, for all in the flesh. Joseph Smith explained that Adam holds special keys because of his role as physical father of all, and also the fact that whenever the keys "are revealed from heaven, it is by Adam's authority."[6]   Adam was the first man among men to be born again and thus "quickened in the inner man," thus becoming the first member of this earth to be adopted into the family of Christ.[7]   Adam held keys as the Presiding Patriarch,[8]   which keys he passed on to his righteous posterity.

Many have supposed that the promises given to the great Patriarch Abraham were one of a kind, and that no other men received the same promises. Yet, the scriptures seem to teach otherwise. In a great revelation on priesthood given in March of 1835, the Lord described the Divine Patriarchal Order and its descent as follows:

> *This order was instituted in the days of Adam, and came down by lineage in the following manner:*
> *From Adam to Seth, who was ordained by Adam at the age of sixty-nine years, and was blessed by him three years previous to his (Adam's) death, and received the promise of God by his father,* that his posterity should be the chosen of the Lord, *and that they should be preserved unto the end of the earth. . . .*[9]

Thus, Seth received from his father the same promise that Abraham received many years later. And so it was with all the Presiding Patriarchs in the lineal descent from Adam to Noah, given in the 107th Section of the *Doctrine and Covenants.*[10]

We are told in scripture that the Prophet Noah was ordained a Patriarch at the tender age of ten years under the hands of Methuselah.[11]   Noah was chosen to be the one to repopulate the earth after the global deluge; it was thus through Noah that all the kingdoms of the earth sprang. In a corrupt and perverted world, Noah found grace in the eyes of the Lord; he was justified to God, was perfect in his generation,[12]   and was thus counted worthy to be part of the Family of Christ.[13]   Noah taught his family the saving principles, such that his sons Ham, Shem and Japheth "walked with God," as did their noble father.[14]   It was the great Prophet Noah who served as the one to restore the fulness of priesthood powers, even the rights of the Divine Patriarchal Order after the time of the flood. The order of Government that existed after the time of the flood was thus patriarchal in nature.[15]   Noah stands among the supreme priesthood figures this side of the flood in time.

The promises of God to the faithful are spelled out most specifically in God's covenant with Abraham. Again, these promises and blessings were and are given to all who become Patriarchs, Kings and Priests to their posterity. First, Abraham was promised an innumerable posterity through all time and eternity; it is important to mention here that this promise was not limited to physical offspring, for note the words of the Lord to Joseph Smith in a revelation received in 1843:

> *Abraham received promises concerning his seed, and of the fruit of his loins—from whose loins ye are, namely, my servant Joseph—which were to continue so long as they were in the world; and as touching Abraham and his seed,* out of the world they should continue; *both in the world and out of the world should they continue as innumerable as the stars; or, if ye were to count the sand upon the seashore ye could not number them.*[16]

Second, the posterity of Abraham are heirs to the Adoption, Glory, and Covenants.[17]   Adoption here refers to adoption into the Family of Christ through subscribing to the Articles of Adoption, or First Principles of the Gospel.[18] The children of Abraham are heirs to the glory of Christ, and thus may receive of His divine powers and influence as He received the same from His Father. To be heirs to the covenants is to have the right to be organized in the Patriarchal Order via the Temple of the Lord. Third, the blessings of this priesthood were to continue in the seed of Abraham through eternity. Thus the Lord explained that ". . .in thee (that is, in thy priesthood) and in thy seed (that is, thy priesthood), for I give unto thee a promise that this right shall continue in thee and in thy seed after thee. . . ."[19]   Fourth, the seed of Abraham were to be the ones to ". . .bear this ministry and priesthood unto all nations.''[20] Through the descendants of Abraham the message of salvation is spread to the world, and thus the powers of the priesthood are actively blessing the lives of those outside the House of Israel. Finally, special priesthood rights were to continue in certain branches of the House of Israel. For example, the rights of the Patriarchal Order descended from Jacob to Ephraim.[21] Ephraim thus has the rights pertaining to the higher sealing powers in the temple.[22] Judah has the rights of political power in the Kingdom.[23] Levi has the right to officiate in the program of the preparatory gospel.[24]

RESTORATION OF KEYS IN THIS DISPENSATION

The rights, powers and keys necessary to establish the Divine Patriarchal Order were restored to the earth in our day on April 3, 1836 in the Kirtland Temple.[25] The coming of the Lord Jesus Christ, and the coming of Moses, Elias, and Elijah to Joseph Smith and Oliver Cowdery mark a glorious day in this latter dispensation, for the keys of the Kingdom were once again committed to man.

After the Lord had appeared and accepted of the Temple as His house and as a place of sacred worship, the record informs us that Moses appeared and committed ''. . .the keys of the gathering of Israel from the four parts of the earth, and the leading of the ten tribes from the land of the north.''[26] The first Elders were thus given the authority and power necessary to gather scattered Israel (including the Lost Tribes) in a day preparatory to the Second Advent. This injunction to gather Israel also included the right to broaden the proselyting efforts, and thus build up the Kingdom of God on earth.

The record explains further that ''After this, Elias appeared, and committed the dispensation of the gospel of Abraham, saying that in us and our seed all generations after us should be blessed.''[27] This messenger, whom

Joseph Smith designated as Elias, we have since learned was the ancient Prophet Noah.[28] Who would be more appropriate as a messenger of restoration than the man who restored the keys of the Patriarchal Order of Priesthood after the flood? The message of Elias (Noah) was a powerful one. Joseph Smith was instructed that through him all the nations of the earth would be blessed. In essence, Joseph received the same promises as Abraham and all of the ancient Patriarchs; Joseph thus stands as a modern Abraham. The magnitude of this covenant is again referred to in a later revelation in which the Lord said: "And as I said unto Abraham concerning the kindreds of the earth, even so I say unto my servant Joseph: In thee and in thy seed shall the kindred of the earth be blessed."[29]   Again the Lord said on another occasion:

> *Abraham received promises concerning his seed, and of the fruit of his loins. . . .*
> *This promise is yours also, because ye are of Abraham, and the promise was made unto Abraham; and by this law is the continuation of the works of my father, wherein he glorifieth himself.*
> Go ye, therefore, and do the works of Abraham; *enter ye into my law and ye shall be saved.* [30]

As early as 1823, Joseph had received revelation relative to the coming of Elijah to bring priesthood keys. In September of 1823 the Prophet Moroni quoted from the fourth chapter of Malachi, with some variation in the original text:

> *Behold, I will* reveal *unto you the Priesthood, by the hand of Elijah the Prophet, before the coming of the great and dreadful day of the Lord.*
> *And he shall plant in the hearts of the children the promises made to the fathers, and the hearts of the children shall turn to their fathers.*

If it were not so, the whole earth would be utterly wasted at his coming. [31]

Elijah the Prophet returned to the earth in 1836, being the last Hebrew prophet to hold the fulness of priesthood power, and thus the keys of the Divine Patriarchal Order. [32] Elijah came to *reveal* an aspect of the priesthood unused by the Prophet Joseph to that point in time. Individuals had been sealed up unto eternal life as early as 1831, [33] but no work had been done with regard to the sealing of families together. Through the keys Elijah restored the promises to Abraham are fulfilled; the hearts of the children thus turn to the fathers, to whom the promises had been made. Joseph Smith later clarified the sealing powers related to this part of the priesthood:

> *What is the office and work of Elijah? It is one of the greatest and most important subjects that God has revealed. He should send Elijah to seal the children to the fathers, and the fathers to the children.* [34]

The question might be asked why the earth would be "utterly wasted" at the coming of the Master if this work (sealing) was not performed. The simple fact is that there would be no permanent connecting ties between parents and children had Elijah not come; in other words, all would be left "without root or branch," [35] or without posterity or ancestry. Obviously the earth would then be an utter waste.

There is some indication that the Modern Seer, Joseph Smith, had full intentions of delegating the Presidency of the Church (Melchizedek Order) to his brother Hyrum, the Patriarch, while he (Joseph) attempted to build up and perfect the Patriarchal Order. Joseph described the situation as follows:

> *Last Monday morning certain men came to me and said: "Brother Joseph, Hyrum is no prophet—he can't*

lead the church. If you resign, all things will go wrong;
you must not resign; if you do the church will be scat-
tered.'' I felt curious and said: ''Have we not learned the
Priesthood after the order of Melchizedek, which includes
both Prophets, Priests and Kings. . . . I will advance your
Prophet to a Priest, and then to a King— *not to the*
Kingdoms of this earth, but of the most High God. . . .''[36]

A sudden death prevented Joseph from fully bringing his
intentions to fruition.

SONS AND DAUGHTERS OF CHRIST

Before any person can become a part of the Divine
Patriarchal Order he must first be born into the Family of
Jesus Christ. Those who are born into the Kingdom of God
through the proper channels become *adopted* into the
Family of the Savior. ''Adoption'' is the act of taking by
choice into some relationship. Having received of the
Fulness of the Father's glory,[37] Christ becomes the means
through which we gain the endowments and powers of the
Spirit, and the only means through which we may gain
eternal life.[38] In an eternal sense, then, He becomes a
Father unto us, inasmuch as we receive life from Him. This
paternal relationship does not exist for all men—only for
those who repent and apply the powers of the Atonement;
those who do not repent are not partakers of His heavenly
gift, and thus not the children of Christ. That those who
walk the strait path become the children of Christ is very
evident in the scriptures. After the people of Zarahemla had
received the great sermon and discourse of King Benjamin,
they all experienced a mighty change, in that they had no
more desire for evil but a great desire to do good continually.[39] They then entered into covenant with the Lord
to stay faithful for the remainder of their days.[40] After
witnessing these proceedings, King Benjamin declared:

> *And now, because of the covenant which ye have made* ye shall be called the children of Christ, *his sons, and his daughters; for behold, this day he hath spiritually begotten you; for ye say that your hearts are changed through faith on his name; therefore, ye are born of him and have become his sons and his daughters.*[41]

In a revelation given to Emma Smith in July of 1830, the Lord said:

> *Hearken unto the voice of the Lord your God, while I speak unto you, Emma Smith, my daughter; for verily I say unto you,* all those who receive my gospel are sons and daughters in my kingdom.[42]

In January of 1831 the word of the Lord came to James Covill as follows:

> *Hearken and listen to the voice of him who is from all eternity to all eternity, the great I AM, even Jesus Christ—*
> *The light and life of the world; a light which shineth in darkness and the darkness comprehendeth it not;*
> *The same which came in the meridian of time unto mine own, and mine own received me not:*
> *But* to as many as received me, gave I power to become my sons; *and even so will I give unto as many as will receive me, power to become my sons.*[43]

Joseph Smith taught that "it is one thing to see the kingdom of God, and another thing to enter into it. We must have a change of heart to see the kingdom of God, and subscribe to articles of adoption to enter therein."[44]   The Articles of Adoption are necessary to be born again and thus become adopted children in the Family of Christ. With Christ as Father and thus the source of eternal life, the just man assumes the position of heir in the Divine Patriarchal Order.

FATHERS AND MOTHERS SPIRITUALLY

Having been born into the Family of Christ and thus become heirs unto Christ, a man must press forward in righteousness to receive greater endowments of glory. It is not intended that a man should remain a child forever; he must mature in the powers of the Spirit until he arrives at the point where he may stand as a spiritual father to his posterity.

Every man and woman who enter the House of the Lord to participate in the covenant of eternal marriage leave that sacred edifice with two major responsibilities, in addition to the obvious covenants entered into therein. First, they have a responsibility to provide mortal tabernacles for the spirit children of the Man of Holiness. Any attempt to prevent, in any artificial way, children from coming into their homes is essentially a form of mockery before God, for this is the major purpose of the new and everlasting covenant of marriage: to raise up seed unto Christ. The second, and most important responsibility is to become fathers and mothers *spiritually* to their children. To be a spiritual father is to be the means whereby the powers of eternal life are transmitted to the offspring. The Temple of the Lord is the only place where a couple may receive the keys to so bless their children. Elder Orson Pratt said:

> Every good principle which you would have your children inherit, should be predominant, and reign in your own bosoms; *for, though the spirits are pure and heavenly when they enter the infant tabernacle, yet they are extremely susceptible of influences, either for good or for bad. The state of the parents' minds at the time of conception, and the state of the mother's mind during her pregnancy, will be constitutionally impressed upon the offspring, bringing with it consequencess which in a degree, have a bearing upon the future destiny of the child.* [45]

President Brigham Young spoke of the responsibility of parents in a similar vein:

> *The father should be full of kindness, and endeavor to happify and cheer the mother, that her heart may be comforted and her affections unimpaired in her earthly protector, that her love for God and righteousness may vibrate throughout her whole being, that she may bear and bring forth offspring impressed and endowed with all the qualities necessary to a being designed to reign king of kings and lord of lords.* [46]

Parents have a mighty responsibility to be holy vessels of the Lord, and the means whereby they may raise up a righteous seed unto Christ. Through the realization of the blessings promised in the House of the Lord, a man stands as a King and a Priest over his posterity; his lovely wife stands as Queen and Priestess. After receiving this glorious appointment, this man and woman stand as God in the resurrection, possessing eternal lives, or the continuation of seeds forever. [47] President Brigham Young taught that in this exalted state man may produce ''both spirit and body.''[48]

> *After men have got their exaltations and their crowns—have become Gods, even the sons of God— are made kings of kings and lords of lords,* they have the power then of propagating their species in spirit. Power is then given to them to organize the elements, and then commence the organization of tabernacles. . . .
> *The Father and the Son have attained to this point already; I am on the way, and so are you, and every faithful servant of God.* [49]

SUMMARY

The Church organization exists to perfect the Saints, continuing to function until we have come to a unity of the faith. There are two orders of the priesthood, each with separate but related tasks. The Melchizedek Order, with its structure of quorums and offices, functions mainly to build the home. The Patriarchal Order is the finished product, the perfected order which will exist throughout eternity. Through the ages the Lord has given the Patriarchal rights to certain valiant men, such as Adam, Seth, Noah, and Abraham. Each of these men received promises that his seed would continue throughout time and eternity, and the powers of this (Patriarchal) Priesthood would continue also. On April 3, 1836 Moses, Elias, and Elijah appeared and revealed the keys necessary to re-establish the Divine Patriarchal Order on the earth; through Joseph Smith all the nations of the earth will be blessed. Men and women may now (through the blessings of the Holy Temple) become fathers and mothers spiritually to their offspring, and thus transmit spiritual powers from one generation to the next. Those who continue faithful will stand as God, enjoying a continuation of seeds forever. In this perfected order, a man stands as a political head (King) and a spiritual leader (Priest) over his posterity.

CHAPTER 8
—FOOTNOTES—

1. See a Conference Report by Joseph F. Smith, April, 1906.
2. TPJS, p. 322
3. JD 3:265-266
4. D & C 107:8
5. TPJS, p. 180
6. TPJS, p. 157, 167
7. Moses 6:65-67
8. D & C 107:40-41
9. *Ibid.,* 107:41-42
10. Some have assumed that each of these men were simply receiving the priesthood for the first time at the ages of 69, 134, 87, etc. However, when read in the true context of this section, verses 39 and 40 make it clear that the verses which follow have reference to the ordination of evangelical ministers or Patriarchs (See also TPJS, p. 151).
11. D & C 107:52; Moses 8:19.

12. Genesis 6:8-9; Moses 8:27
13. Moses 8:13
14. Genesis 6:9; Moses 8:27
15. Abraham 1:25-26
16. D & C 132:30
17. Romans 9:4; TPJS, p. 189
18. See TPJS, p. 328
19. Abraham 2:11
20. *Ibid.*, 2:9
21. See 1 Chronicles 5:1-2; Jeremiah 31:9
22. D & C 133:32; see also JD 4:231-232; JD 18:38
23. Genesis 49:10
24. Exodus 30:30-31; Ibid., 40:13-15
25. D & C 110
26. *Ibid.*, 110:11
27. *Ibid.*, 110:12
28. Compare D & C 27:7 and TPJS, p. 157
29. D & C 124:58
30. *Ibid.*, 132:30-32
31. D & C 2: Compare Malachi 4:5-6
32. See TPJS, pp. 172, 337
33. The Doctrine of Sealing in this latter dispensation was undertaken in Chapter 3.
34. TPJS, p. 337
35. See Malachi 4:1
36. TPJS, p. 318
37. D & C 93:16
38. *Ibid.*, 93:19-20
39. Mosiah 5:1-2
40. *Ibid.*, 5:5
41. *Ibid.*, 5:7
42. D & C 25:1
43. *Ibid.*, 39:1-3
44. TPJS, p. 328
45. *The Seer*, pp. 155-156
46. JD 8:62
47. D & C 132:19-20
48. JD 15:137
49. JD 6:275

BIBLIOGRAPHY AND SUGGESTED READINGS

Allen, Edward J. *The Second United Order Among the Mormons.* New York: Ams Press, 1967.

Andrus, Hyrum L. *Joseph Smith and World Government.* Salt Lake City: Deseret Book Company, 1958.

Andrus, Hyrum L. *Doctrinal Commentary on the Pearl of Great Price.* Salt Lake City: Deseret Book Company, 1967.

Andrus, Hyrum L. *Principles of Perfection.* Salt Lake City: Bookcraft, 1970.

Andrus, Hyrum L. *Descriptions of Zion.* Salt Lake City: Hawkes Publishing Inc., 1973

Andrus, Hyrum L. *Doctrines of the Kingdom.* Salt Lake City: Bookcraft, 1973.

Arrington, Leonard J. "Early Mormon Communitarianism: The Law of Consecration and Stewardship," *Western Humanities Review, VII (Autumn 1953).*

Arrington, Leonard J. *Great Basin Kingdom.* Cambridge: Harvard University Press, 1958.

Callis, Charles A. in *Conference Report of the Church of Jesus Christ of Latter-day Saints,* April, 1923.

Christiansen, ElRay L. "A Foundation Stone of the Gospel," *Improvement Era* 65:957 (December, 1962).

Clark, J. Reuben, Jr. in *Conference Report of the Church of Jesus Christ of Latter-day Saints,* October 1942.

Cleland, Robert G. and Juanita Brooks (eds.) *A Mormon Chronicle: The diaries of John D. Lee, 1848-1876.* 2 vols. San Marino, California, 1955.

Cowley, Matthias F. *Wilford Woodruff.* Salt Lake City: Bookcraft, 1964.

Crowther, Duane S. *Prophecy—Key to the Future.* Salt Lake City: Bookcraft, 1962.

Doxey, Roy W. *Zion in the Last Days.* Salt Lake City: Bookcraft, 1968.

Durham, G. Homer. *The Gospel Kingdom: Selections from the Writings and Discourses of John Taylor.* Salt Lake City: Bookcraft, 1964.

Dyer, Alvin R. *The Refiner's Fire.* Salt Lake City: Deseret Book Company, 1972.

Evening and Morning Star (Independence, Missouri), I (July 1832).

Geddes, Joseph A. *The United Order Among the Mormons.* Salt Lake City: The Deseret News Press, 1924.

Hansen, Klaus J. "The Political Kingdom of God as a Cause for Mormon-Gentile Conflict," *Brigham Young University Studies*, II (Spring - Summer 1960).

Hansen, Klaus J. *Quest for Empire.* Michigan State University Press, 1967.

Hill, Marvin S. and James B. Allen (eds). *Mormonism and American Culture.* New York: Harper & Row, 1972.

Holt, James. "The Reminiscenses of James Holt. A Narrative of the Emmett Company," ed. Dale Morgan, *Utah Historical Quarterly*, XXV (1957).

Ivins, Stanley S. "Notes on Mormon Polygamy," *Western Humanities Review*, X (Summer 1956).

Johnson, Benjamin F. to George S. Gibbs, April-October 1903 (typed manuscript, Brigham Young University Library).

Journal of Discourses. 26 vols. London: Latter-day Saints' Book Depot, 1854-1886.

Kimball, Heber C. *Prophetic Sayings of Heber C. Kimball to Amanda H. Wilcox,* Brigham Young University Library.

Lee, Harold B. in *Conference Report of the Church of Jesus Christ of Latter-day Saints,* October 1961, April 1963.

Lee, John D. *Mormonism Unveiled.* St. Louis: 1877.

Lightner, Mary. *The Life and Testimony of Mary Lightner.* Dugway: Pioneer Press, n.d.

Ludlow, Daniel H. *Latter-day Prophets Speak*. Salt Lake City: Bookcraft, 1951.

Lund, Gerald N. *The Coming of the Lord*. Salt Lake City: Bookcraft, 1971.

Lundwall, N. B. compiler. *Temples of the Most High*. Salt Lake City: Bookcraft, 1968.

McConkie, Bruce R. *Mormon Doctrine*. 2nd ed. Salt Lake City: Bookcraft, 1966.

"Minutes of the Council of Fifty, 1880" (Brigham Young University Library).

"Minutes of the School of the Prophets Held in Parowan 1868-1872." Manuscript in Brigham Young University Library. Typewritten copy, 1956.

Mouritsen, Dale C. "The Relationship of the Priesthood Correlation Program to the Latter-day Saint Concept of Zion." Master's thesis, Brigham Young University, 1968.

Nelson, Lowrey. *The Mormon Village*. Salt Lake City: University of Utah Press, 1952.

Patrick, John R. "The School of the Prophets: Its Development and Influence in Utah Territory." Master's thesis, Brigham Young University, 1970.

Pratt, Orson. "The Kingdom of God." *Millennial Star*, 10:305-309, 321-324 (15 October, 1 November 1848).

Pratt, Orson. *The Seer*. Washington D.C., 1854.

Pratt, Orson. *The Holy Spirit*. Liverpool, 1856.

Pratt, Parley P. *A Voice of Warning*. new ed. Salt Lake City: The Church of Jesus Christ of Latter-day Saints, 1957.

"Proclamation of the Twelve Apostles of the Church of Jesus Christ of Latter-day Saints," *Millennial Star*, October 22, 1845.

Robison, Parker Pratt. *Writings of Parley Parker Pratt*. Salt Lake City: Deseret News Press, 1952.

Romney, Marion G. "Socialism and the United Order Compared," *Improvement Era*, 69:535-538 (June 1966).

128

Royall, Paul F. *Every Man in His Place*....Discourse at Brigham Young University Six-Stake Fireside, January 3, 1965. Provo, Utah: Brigham Young University Press, 1965.

Skousen, W. Cleon. *Prophecy and Modern Times*. Salt Lake City: Deseret Book, 1939.

Smith, Joseph. *History of the Church of Jesus Christ of Latter-day Saints*. Edited by B. H. Roberts. 2nd ed. rev. 7 vols. Salt Lake City: Deseret Book, 1964.

Smith, Joseph F. *Conference Report of the Church of Jesus Christ of Latter-day Saints*, April 1906.

Smith, Joseph F. *Gospel Doctrine*. Salt Lake City: The Deseret News, 1919.

Smith, Joseph Fielding. *The Way to Perfection*. Salt Lake City: The Genealogical Society, 1933.

Smith, Joseph Fielding. *Teachings of the Prophet Joseph Smith*. Salt Lake City: Deseret Book, 1938.

Smith, Joseph Fielding. *Doctrines of Salvation*. 3 vols. Salt Lake City: Bookcraft, 1954-1956.

Talmage, James E. *Articles of Faith*. Salt Lake City: The Church of Jesus Christ of Latter-day Saints, 1960.

Taylor, John. *The Government of God*. London: The LDS Book Depot, 1852.

Whitney, Orson F. "The Aaronic Priesthood." *The Contributor*, VI (October 1884).

Widstoe, John A. *Discourses of Brigham Young*. Salt Lake City: Deseret Book, 1954.

Widstoe, John A. *Priesthood and Church Government*. Rev. ed. Salt Lake City: Deseret Book, 1954.

Young, Joseph. *History of the Organization of the Seventies*. Salt Lake City: Deseret News Steam Printing Establisment, 1878.

Young Woman's Journal, Vol. 16 (December 1905).